WORTH EVERYTHING

Why Your Self-Esteem Should Flow From God

FRANK CASSO

WORTH EVERYTHING
Why Your Self-Esteem Should Flow from God

Copyright © 2015 Frank Casso

Inquiries should be addressed by email to
Frank Casso
WorthEverything@MyTestimony.com

ISBN-13: 978-1-941280-02-7
ISBN-10: 1941280021

Published by CEFO Publications

All scriptures used are from the King James Version
of the Holy Bible. Out of reverence and respect, all pronoun
references pertaining to God the Father and the Lord Jesus
Christ have been capitalized.

Printed in the United States of America.

DEDICATION

This book is dedicated to Believers everywhere who have struggled with who they are, and who they hope to be. May God impart to you an immovable and unshakeable understanding that you are His, through the Lord Jesus Christ.

TABLE OF CONTENTS

FOREWORD

As a Christian, I personally am constantly exploring and contemplating new ways to become more Christ-like. Admittedly, even after sufficient revelation and study, oftentimes I am unexceptional in my efforts in the best case scenario, and a disappointment to myself at worst. Yet I know that the Word says that we shall someday be like Him (I John 3:2). It is our spiritual destiny to become more like Jesus as we mature and grow in the Lord. But what does that look like here in this life? Can we somehow partake of that in the here and now?

It is my contention that we Christians are often plagued and harangued by the worst versions of ourselves. We fail to break free from the condemnation we feel for our lack of effort, our lack of understanding, our lack of obedience to God. We falter, fail, and dishonor our witness because we are tempted by sin, goaded by the enemy, and hopelessly entangled in our own demeaning self-images. How can we be the best witnesses for Christ when we often feel and believe that we are the worst examples of Christianity?

This is the dreadful trap that we must escape. Yet, even with all our might, with all our efforts, is it possible to ever break free from that?

I believe that if you seek the Holy Spirit's guidance and spiritual revelation, I am certain that you will see that there is abundant biblical evidence to support the premise which is offered in this book. That is, that God is the provider and supporter of our self-esteem. He is the Redeemer of it. We should look to Him to help us understand why our sense of self-worth should come from Jesus, and not from ourselves. Our self-worthiness must be derived only from how God regards us; and not from any person, event, achievement, or challenge. In fact, we should not even deign to regard our own selves, without Him as the originator and preserver of our self-esteem.

We challenge and encourage you to "step outside of yourself" and attempt to see a spiritually reborn and ever-learning child of God; rather than as a failure or a mediocre follower of Christ. As you read on, I hope you are persuaded that *who you are* is not defined by what you do, what others say, or any other typically accepted measure. In addition, how you see yourself should not depend at all on you, but rather it must depend solely and wholly upon Christ.

That is why we proclaim that your self-esteem should flow from God.

PREFACE

Self-esteem comes from within yourself. It is based on your set of beliefs and your conscious thoughts, behaviors, feelings and actions. It is determined by how you view and consider your place, purpose, and value in this life.

But exactly how is self-esteem generated? How do we get it? How do we keep and maintain it? Why does it sometimes seem to arrive unintentionally, only to then abruptly disappear? And why is it even important? After all, it's just a feeling, isn't it? Feelings come and go, but why is self-esteem the one personal and internal attribute that can permeate our entire being, to the point of powerfully affecting our decisions, our actions, and our behaviors?

If self-esteem could be converted to pennies, there would be some people who have truckloads; while others might barely carry a handful. If a personal self-esteem meter were available to us, such as a "health-meter" found in a video game, some people would be at or near the max amount—in the green, if you will. But just like players in a video game, there are those who are constantly searching for a self-esteem "power-up" or boost—perpetually needing to find a hidden cache of self-worth because their meter is always running low or stalled on empty.

This book is aimed at Christians whose self-opinion is not clear. Many of us are regularly bouncing back and forth in the "red to yellow zones" of the aforementioned self-worth meter. We feel okay with our lives on various levels, but we know things could be better—*we* could be better. We struggle daily with the demands and chores of daily life, much like everyone else. Yet in the back of our minds, we're always cognizant of the fact that God is on our side, and we're blessed (or maybe just lucky) to have a relationship with the Almighty. Often, that is good enough for us.

But is it good enough for God?

"WHAT?" you ask. "What is that supposed to mean? God is *GOD*. I'm just me. There's no way that I could meet His expectations anyway–at least, not in this lifetime. I mean, isn't that what Salvation is all about—the mercy and grace of God—taking care of what I could never earn or buy? Believe me, right now I'm just trying to be a good and decent Christian, doing what I can do to further the Kingdom of the Lord. I'm giving it my best, just hoping I don't mess up His plans too much in the process. Sometimes I get it right, sometimes I don't. He understands that because He is gracious and merciful, *isn't He?*"

Yes, He is. He does understand. And that is precisely why He has made provisions for His children in every area of life. He has made a way to give us eternal life through Jesus Christ.

Sidebar: If you are not sure you are a Christian, please turn right now to the chapter titled *"Your Salvation: Worth Everything."* Read the chapter and pray the prayer of repentance. If you are honest and sincere with yourself—and with God—He will save you and give you eternal life. Please don't put it off. He loves you and wants to spend a joyous future with you.

Thankfully, God has generously and graciously included provision for self-esteem, as He has provided so many other blessings as well. As we progress through the coming chapters, you will learn:

1. Why our self-esteem is important to God.
2. Why He has provided us with an ample supply of self-worth.
3. How our self-esteem, as provided by God, can positively affect our actions and decisions.
4. Why and how our self-value should never be linked to what we do, or how we look, or what others think of us, or our personal achievements (or lack thereof), or any other worldly influence or measure.
5. How our feelings impact our self-esteem.

As we begin to embark on this new and exciting journey of discovery, we must first establish certain absolutes. These will serve as the bedrock for our entire discussion on self-esteem. They are based on the most basic and fundamental of Christian principles. Many will be familiar in some regards, while others will be alien to your thinking. In any case, it will be up to you to decide if and how you will incorporate them into your thoughts and being. Let us state that the Holy Spirit will help you determine whether or not these truths are certain and evident. We are confident that if you sincerely seek God's guidance and clarity, then you will come to a common knowledge with us, and therefore more readily receive the remaining aspects of this book.

Further, we will support each point with substantive logic and information, which will be derived from the Word of God, the Holy Bible.

1

THERE ARE ABSOLUTES

Throughout history, and most especially today, the secular world has tried its best to renounce God, faith, the story of Creation, the plan of Salvation, the Bible, etc. More often than not, the ultimate objective in attacking these tenets is meant to dispense with the notion that God exists, and that He will eventually hold us all accountable. The very fact that the world has worked so hard at this for virtually all of human history is, in fact, a sort of testament that He does exist. For what would be served in devoting so much time, money, effort, political power, and blood to destroying a fantasy? However, because you as a Christian have already embraced the idea that He is real, that Jesus is the Son of God, and that He fulfilled God's plan for saving mankind, we shall begin this study from that starting point.

"For God so loved the world that He gave His only begotten Son, that whosoever believeth on Him should not perish, but have everlasting life." (John 3:16)

It is this fundamental scripture and its foundational belief upon which we shall build.

So we must first ask, do you believe John 3:16 is true? Of course you do. It's true because it's in the Bible, God's written Word to us. You also know it's true because **you** are the living proof that it is so. You believe in Jesus, and so you now believe that you have everlasting life. And where is this truth found? Of course . . . it's in the Bible—a collection of written histories, letters and poetry written by men—yet inspired by God.

Every Christian will attest John 3:16 is true. Individuals of every race, and from every culture and corner of this earth, have come to know God in a personal way through this powerful, yet tender-loving verse of scripture. It is probably safe to assume that this one passage of the Bible has played a direct part in the salvation of countless millions. (This author is included among them.) God infused His intent and love into this particular verse of scripture. He has preserved its true meaning for all generations since it was first written. The simplicity and power of the message has never changed, nor has it been diluted down to a lesser version of itself. God Himself has seen to its preservation through the ages by protecting the words and substance of what He intended.

So now we must ask the next reasonable question: is it probable, or more accurately, is it not actually a _certainty_, that He has done the same for the rest of His Word? Or are we to surmise that the remainder of God's Word, unlike this specific verse, is subject to changes, re-imaginations, or modifications? Ultimately, the question we are asking here is, "Is God's entire Word—_the Bible_—true or not? And if it is, then is it _completely true_—or not? This is not an insignificant question. It deserves careful and thoughtful consideration, and the answer must be profoundly clear and irrefutable.

Let me ask you, do you believe that the Almighty God is capable of protecting His Word from the selfish or arrogant intentions of mere men who might try to contort or pervert it? I hope that you do. But, if your answer is no, then how can you know that John 3:16 is true; remaining unspoiled and pure in its meaning? If it is not true, then we must deny the evidence in our own lives that He has saved us, and set us free from the power of sin. This is a weighty matter to consider. These questions are posed to you not just to challenge your thinking on this particular verse. It is for the purpose of establishing an absolute that you may not have considered before in this light or from this perspective. It is intended to carry forward your thinking and understanding in a way that you may not have previously considered.

The very fact that your mind has been freed from the torments of guilt and sin is proof that this verse is true. The evidence that you have been physically healed, delivered from oppression, set free from drugs or other addictions are all confirmations of John 3:16. Your marriage has been restored, your relationships healed, your mind set free, your guilt and shame nullified—these all verify what you know to be true. So let us all praise God that John 3:16 is indeed true! And praise God that He's *big enough, smart enough, strong enough*, and *wise enough* to protect and preserve His Word—***all of it***—for all generations.

"All scripture is given by inspiration of God, and is profitable for doctrine, for reproof, for correction, for instruction in righteousness." (II Timothy 3:16)

> Sidebar: We don't claim that there aren't difficulties in understanding certain aspects of scripture. There are specific instances in the Bible that, on the surface, seem to be contradictory. But we must trust that God will give us understanding and reveal these mysteries to us as we continue to mature and grow in Him. The entire Bible isn't written as a collection of unsolvable puzzles, riddles, and mysteries. Much of it is plainspoken and straightforward, perhaps even the majority of it. So let's just accept it as whole truth, and move forward with that. We don't need to understand or explain every seemingly opposing thought or event. God is still going to honor His Word <u>as He sees fit</u>, whether we thoroughly understand it or not. Don't let that stop you from fully believing and trusting in His Word.

So, you may ask, "Why is it necessary to establish *this* point? Even if I concede that all of God's Word is true, I thought this book was going to help me learn about self-esteem?" And so it shall, but we must firmly settle in our own minds that since God's Word is true in one area (e.g., Salvation), then it will also be true in others. We must confirm that God has the power and willingness to preserve His Word throughout the ages—*all of it*. Only then can we realize and accept the remaining truths that are presented and evident throughout His Word.

Now, the idea that your self-esteem is something that God has ordained for you is a new concept to many Believers. We want you to get comfortable with that as we explain and support it with Scripture. These verses will be no less valid than John 3:16, for God has preserved His intentions in them as well.

To begin, let us look more closely at what tends to affect how we view, as well as what we think, about ourselves.

As we stated earlier, self-esteem comes from within yourself, based on your set of beliefs and your conscious thoughts, behaviors, feelings and actions. It is how you view yourself and how you consider your place and purpose in this life. This is key to any sense of personal value. But how do we create, and then maintain, that value if we don't know how that is done? How do we add to it, protect it, and keep it strong?

Let's personally reflect for a moment. Perhaps since you became saved, you have still thought about yourself or acted in one of the following ways:

I can't stand myself.
I'm not attractive.
I'm not very smart.
My body's too weird.
I never have any money.
I don't have a good education.
I don't have any friends.
I drive an old car.
I have no real talents.
I'm just a nobody.

No one cares about me, so why should I care about myself?
Why should I try for that job? They don't want somebody like me.
I'm going to hurt myself, then maybe someone will notice me.
Who cares if I drink too much? I don't care.
I can't believe I did drugs again.
I promised myself that I wouldn't lie anymore. Why did I do it?

I can't stop myself. Why does my life have to be so hard?

It's no wonder that our self-esteem is so low. We're

"supposed to be Christians", yet at times we feel small, unloved, and useless. We manage to foul up time and time again. We can't seem to stay steady and strong in the face of adversity, temptation, or affliction. And even when we genuinely seek help and forgiveness from God, our past actions and attitudes continue to color and affect our thoughts and behaviors. We *want* to be a better Christian, and we may be for a while, but we can't ever seem to *stay* better. The guilt, shame, and disappointment arising from our shortcomings affect us in everything. It eventually becomes a circuitous trap with no means of escape.

We feel bad about ourselves.
We yield to temptation and sin.
We regret our thoughts and actions, and repent.
We continue to feel bad about ourselves because we failed God.
We start all over again.

With no clear end to this entangled type of thinking, we are doomed to repeat the very things that destroy our self-esteem. It is the legendary and mythical "catch-22". Even if we successfully disengage from this circular snare for a season, as soon as we falter, we are back in as deeply as we ever were. It is no wonder that our sense of self-worth suffers so.

So, how to break free?

To answer this, we must ask ourselves two very important questions.

The first one is, "How did you break free the first time?"

Truly, the answer is so very simple, most of us think it can't possibly be that easily addressed again. We all know that asking God for forgiveness is what initially set us free. Jesus intended for us to have "*life more abundantly.*" (John 10:10) We have all experienced that sensation or awareness that the shackles of our past sins and behaviors have truly been broken, and their grip on our lives is no more. For some of us, it was instantaneous; for others more gradual. Yet it came nevertheless, and it clearly came from God through the Lord Jesus Christ. Thank God for His mercy!

So then, the answer to the question on how to break free is . . . <u>ask God to forgive you</u>. Yes, it really is that uncomplicated. We have often heard it expressed this way:

*"For heaven's sake, when you mess up, run **to** Jesus, don't run away from Him."*

We all think that because we willfully and intentionally sinned, effectively flouting God's forgiveness and love, that there must be something else we must do—some sort of penance we must endure. And because we don't know what His punishment for our failing should be, we tend to impose our own forms of self-punishment which we believe in some way, will measure up to our sin. We may begin to loathe ourselves because we were so weak. We might indulge in the same sinful behavior (or other types of sin) because we believe that we've "blown it anyway". We might shun our prayer time or church fellowship to keep from reminding ourselves of the guilt and shame we feel. Or we might dive even deeper into sin's quagmire, full of regret and remorse; unable to save ourselves, much less help others.

It is all just a skillful trap of the enemy. To be sure, God definitely wants us to live holy and sanctified lives, but He is still willing to help you when you fail. He doesn't want you to stay bound up in sin, He wants you to be truly free from it. And that is why He forgave you in the first place. Do you suppose that if He did that for you once, He might be willing to do it for you again?

But you don't understand! You don't know what I did! How can I call myself a Christian after what I've done? There is no way that God could ever forgive me, especially because I knew that what I was doing was wrong, but I went ahead and did it anyway. I just can't imagine that God is okay with that.

He is not okay with it, nor will He ever be. When temptation or troubles came to you, He would rather that you had taken your rightful authority over that situation, and rejected it in Jesus' name. But you didn't. And now He has to decide whether or not the two of you can continue to have a relationship. Do you now believe that it is possible that your sin has destroyed that relationship? Have you singlehandedly undone the powerful work of Salvation through Jesus Christ by your selfish and sinful words or deeds?

> Sidebar: Before man ever even existed, before the foundations of the world, God had devised a wonderful plan to redeem His creation because He already knew what man's inclination toward sin would be. God wanted to rescue man from his own self-destructive destiny. He planned ahead for that very reason. (Note: The intricacies and covert nature of the Plan of Redemption are in and of themselves, worthy of extensive study and personal meditation. But for our purposes here, we will just acknowledge and accept them as they are.) God had the whole thing measured, calculated, and weighed out to the very last detail. Every sin—every sin of every kind, of every person who will ever exist—was taken care of, covered and then washed away by the Blood of Jesus. That's God's generosity and grace at its very best.

But now, somehow, you as a professed Christian, have given in to some form of temptation and sin, and BOOM! Your relationship with God is over, blown to bits by your behavior; your salvation is now totally and completely wrecked and undone. The powerful and intricate work of Redemption has been obliterated in an instant. Sounds overly dramatic, but let's not understate this. According to this type of thinking, you are now no longer saved and/or in God's good graces because you have sinned. Is that not what has happened here?

Now take a moment and seriously ponder this carefully: Do you suppose that it is terribly vainglorious to think that _you_—solely by the fact that you yielded to sinful behavior, perhaps even purposely engaged in it—are able to utterly destroy God's power to redeem you from eternal damnation?

Amazing! Where did you get such power? What has made you believe that you have the authority and ability to wreck, and then actually negate God's saving grace? And exactly when and how did the Father relinquish His control over eternal justice?

As farfetched as this sounds, there are many Christians who genuinely believe they can nullify God's ability to save them. They just haven't articulated it or thought about it in exactly this way. Yet the Bible tells us the following:

"_All things were made by Him; and without Him was not any thing made that was made._" (John 1:3)
"_Shall the thing formed say to Him that formed it, 'Why hast thou made me thus'? Hath not the potter power over the clay?_" (Romans 9:21)

Therefore, if Christians would just stop and contemplate for a moment: The Lord created all things—*everything*. We were not consulted; nor were we asked for advice, guidance, or consent in any of God's plan. (If you take a moment to think about and analyze that honestly, you'll realize that's actually a good thing.) And among all of God's designs, He foresaw trouble ahead for man, and put into place a rescue plan for His most prized of creations. So He created a plan to redeem us. He had to do that because He knew man would falter and fail by making the wrong choices and the wrong decisions. But He loved man and wanted to save him. So, the plan of Redemption was devised by God—who also created the same man, Adam, who would eventually sin. We are descendants of that man. We did not create ourselves. We cannot save ourselves. And most importantly, we cannot *un-save* ourselves. How could anyone be convinced that they hold the power to "un-save" themselves, when they never had the power to "save" themselves in the first place? Think carefully about that for a moment.

We must also realize that we do not have the authority or power to question why He has done it this way. (We are the clay, remember?) We can only choose to accept redemption and forgiveness, or reject it. However, with this point made, there is one major potential pitfall that has become a genuine stumbling block for many Christians.

Individuals, as well as entire denominations have discussed, disagreed, and had heated debates over what some call a "once saved, always saved" ideology.

At first glance, it may appear that our discussion here supports that concept. Whether we personally do or do not is not at issue. The primary point we are actually making here is somewhat related, but still different. Once again, our contention is that we, as created beings have never had—do not now have— nor will we ever have—the power to save or un-save ourselves. *Our only power is having the choice to make a personal decision—to either accept Jesus, or to reject Him.* The spiritual mechanics of how Salvation occurs, and what transpires to effectively activate and maintain it is entirely and unequivocally in the Father's hands. Essentially, our argument here is that it's up to God, *and only God*, to determine how to make it all work. And our position is, that somehow, in some way, He **does** have it all figured out. To presume that the Lord God Almighty absentmindedly overlooked how our subsequent actions could jeopardize or undermine His plans for redeeming us and our salvation is almost comical to consider.

To summarize, as the Creator of everything (John 1:3), God undoubtedly has always had the authority to save. He retains that authority still. He has not now, *nor will He ever*, consign this ability and privilege to anyone other than the Son.

"For I am persuaded, that neither death nor life. . . nor powers, nor things present, nor things to come . . . shall be able to separate us from the love of God, which is in Christ Jesus." (Romans 8:38-39)

13

Sidebar: One more aspect of this is worth referencing before we go any further. Some would interpret our assertion as an open-ended license for a Christian to sin. They may argue, "If you can't un-save yourself, then you can do whatever you want and still be accepted by God." Perhaps. But know and understand this: the creation cannot scam the Creator. *"For the Word of God . . . is a discerner of the thoughts and intents of the heart."* (Hebrews 4:12) He knows if you were genuine in your original surrendering to Christ. We further contend that **you**, in your innermost being, will know. In addition, there are various spiritual precautions and protections that God has put into place that will make it more and more difficult for a Christian to willfully and purposefully engage in unbridled sin. (The primary safeguard to help you turn away from sin is God's Holy Spirit. There are others, but once again, they all deserve their own study and meditation time.)

Hopefully, we have now firmly and solidly established that your salvation is a spiritual event over which only God has all power and authority. That is, of course, once *you* have chosen to ask for forgiveness of your sins, and received that in faith.

So the second question we need to consider is about the actions you take following your sinful behavior. Specifically, whatever sin(s) you have engaged in at any time *after* your moment of salvation. That question is this:

Precisely when do you think God becomes aware of your failing?

Once again, the answer here is simple and straightforward. God—our Creator, and the Creator of all things seen and unseen—is aware of your sin at the very instant it occurs. Some say that He is already aware of *all* of your sins—past, present, and future— and that is why His forgiveness is so far-reaching and all-encompassing. This is based on the concept that God exists outside of the limits of linear time, (Time can neither contain nor constrain Him. He created it, remember?) so it is perfectly logical to presume that He has knowledge of all that is to come.

Sidebar: Some will argue that God's foreknowledge supports the idea of pre-destination, i.e., that certain people are pre-selected by Him to be saved over those He has already doomed. This is a very deep and serious question that requires thoughtful study and revelation from God. Our position here is that when John 3:16 states *"whosoever believeth"*, it is a clear and irrefutable invitation to anyone *and* everyone to accept Jesus as their Lord and Savior. This verse alone makes it difficult to sustain the idea that God has purposefully chosen some that He wants to save, and others He chooses to condemn.

In either case, because God carefully and thoughtfully pre-planned for the removal of sin from those who choose Jesus, it is rather short-sighted of us to think that He somehow overlooked the probability that a born-again Christian might actually sin *after* their salvation moment, and thus imperil their own redemption. Therefore, we should once again presume the infinite wisdom and goodness of God, realizing that He must have considered this, and thus provided a solution for this very probable and likely scenario.

Paul himself gives us an inside angle on the heart of God as it pertains to this concept. Long after his own salvation event, he refers to himself in the following ways:

"Jesus came . . . to save sinners; of whom I am chief." (I Timothy 1:15)
"Oh, wretched man that I am!" (Romans 7:24)

Paul clearly struggled with guilt, temptation, and sin after his conversion. Yet instead of lamenting his loss of redemption and eternal salvation, he encouraged us through his own example, indicating that the Lord's grace and mercy can, *and will*, rescue us from ourselves. If Paul had succeeded in voiding his own salvation because of sin, then he would not have stated in II Timothy 4:7-8, *"I have fought a good fight, I have finished my course, I have kept the faith: Henceforth there is laid up for me a crown of righteousness . . ."* These were among his last recorded words before his death. They are surely not the words of a defeated and beaten man whose eternal future holds nothing but everlasting condemnation and torment.

So then, *"If we confess our sins, He is faithful and just to forgive us our sins, and to cleanse us from all unrighteousness."* (I John 1:9) This was written <u>*to Christians*</u> to remind us that God *wants* to forgive our sins. He is not holding back in His desire to relieve us from sin's constraints and influences.

<u>Sidebar</u>: It is Adam's original sin that resulted in spiritual death for succeeding generations. Jesus is the last Adam (see I Corinthians 15:45-49), and He has restored us from spiritual death (i.e., eternal separation from God) to life everlasting in His presence. In other words, <u>your</u> own personal sins are derivatives and the results of the spiritual death brought on by Adam's original sin. (By the way, simply ceasing to engage in all sinful activity, if such a thing were even possible for us to do, is not enough to reverse that effect. The damage caused by Adam's sin alone condemned all of mankind, and is irreparable without Jesus.) All of your sins prior to a personal salvation event are characteristic of that spiritual death. But when a Believer becomes "born again", their spirit is restored from death to life, as they are adopted into the family of God, and are now able to call Him *"Abba, Father"* (Romans 8:15). This is critical in that whatever sins we may commit after our individual salvation event, they cannot undo what Jesus has restored as the last Adam. However, if we allow it, these sins can cause us to wallow in self-pity, self-loathing, guilt, and shame—which effectively neutralizes our ability to fellowship with God as He desires and intends.

The story of the Prodigal son bears this out (Luke 11:15-32). Of course the father was overjoyed to see his son return home. But the hidden message is that even when caught up in the heights of revelry, rebellion, and sin, the son **NEVER** ceased to be the son. That biological, spiritual, and love connection could not be severed. So it is with us and our heavenly Father. It may be that we wander from God's love and fellowship by indulging in sin and transgressions, but as an adopted heir and joint-heir with Jesus Christ (Romans 8:17), we never cease to be God's child.

So then it is incumbent on us to confess our sins, after which God forgives us, and then separates our sin from us; "*As far as the east is from the west, so far that He removeth our transgressions from us.*" (Psalm 103:12) As any good mathematician will tell you—that is essentially one linear infinity headed away and directly opposite from, another linear infinity. This means that the two components (you and your sins) will never, ever meet again! Micah 7:19 also states, "*He will turn again, He will have compassion upon us; He will subdue our iniquities; and thou wilt cast all their sins into the depths of the sea.*" This is another very clear indication of His intentions towards us. He **wants** to forgive us, and never *ever* remember our failings again!

I'm pretty sure God has a *very* good memory. In fact, I will unequivocally state that God is *not capable* of forgetting anything. But if He says to us, "*I, even I, am He that blotteth out thy transgressions for mine own sake, and will not remember thy sins,*" (Isaiah 43:25) then He has *intentionally* forgotten our sins. So, who are we to remind Him? Moreover, if God cannot be reminded of something that He has literally expunged from existence, why should we expend any effort in reminding ourselves? And taken one step further, who is satan to remind us? We are both part of God's creation, and cannot countermand or disregard His decision or pronouncement on this matter.

The Creator has effectively declared, "Here's how I'm going to handle this sin business" and that should settle it. So we must ask again, by what right, or by what authority, do we have to accuse ourselves further? Similarly, by what right or by what authority does the enemy have to accuse us? The point here is: once you have earnestly sought forgiveness from God, as far as the Almighty is concerned, it is forgiven and forgotten; it is over and done with. There is no reason to discuss the sin further, since God has completely and thoroughly wiped it away.

Sidebar: We must all realize, however, that sin will have natural consequences, or rather consequences in our natural world. For example, a drug dealer may be arrested and imprisoned for his or her actions. An adulterous man or woman could suffer the end of their marriage or loss of their family. A habitual liar or gossiper might be exposed for their behavior and shunned because of a loss of trust. If the Christian engages in sinful behavior, and then they sincerely seek God's forgiveness, He will most definitely forgive them. However, the natural repercussions of their actions may still need to be addressed or satisfied in

---

some way. God may miraculously intervene, to remove or reduce any penalty for the sinful actions. But that effect would only occur by the grace and wisdom of God, and available at His sole discretion. Otherwise, the transgression may carry with it a natural punishment or aftermath that could have been avoided if the sin itself had never occurred. (Examples: Loss of a job because of illegal or unethical activity; a child born out of wedlock or an adulterous affair (incidentally, the child is faultless in this scenario and deserves to be loved and nurtured); a broken friendship because of gossip or backbiting, etc.) Surely, this entire topic merits much more extensive study, but the goal here is to clearly state that sin may have deeper natural consequences, and as Christians, we should always be wary of the potentially high costs to ourselves and others. Perhaps that sobering thought should act as another deterrent for us to consider when we are faced with tempting opportunities to sin.

In conclusion, let us quickly review these absolutes:

1. God has preserved His intentions in John 3:16.
2. If God can/does preserve His intentions in John 3:16, then by extension, it is reasonable to presume He would preserve the remainder of His Word.
3. People's sins are forgiven when they become a Christian.
4. Christians will commit sin at some point after their salvation event.

5. God was aware of our propensity to sin (even after our personal salvation event), and made provisions to redeem us anyway.
6. We alone do not have the power to save or unsave ourselves.
7. God forgets our sin when we ask for forgiveness, and no one has the right to accuse us with them ever again.

These spiritual principles will serve as the backdrop for our study in self-esteem. If you accept our analyses, then please read on. If you do not, then we suggest that you stop here, single out the topic(s) which you question or with which you disagree. Then do your own due diligence. Pray and ask the Holy Spirit for wisdom, guidance, and revelation. Search the Word for everything you can find on the subject, no matter how unrelated it may first appear to be. James wrote that *"If any of you lack wisdom, let him ask of God, that giveth to all men liberally . . ."* (James 1:5) God wants you to understand Him better, and to know and understand your place in His Son's Kingdom. He isn't trying to hide knowledge from you.

He wants you to know who you are *because of Him.*

2

WHY IS MY SELF-ESTEEM IMPORTANT TO GOD?

The world tells us how it defines self-esteem. Or more accurately, what it wants you to believe is important so that you will measure your self-esteem by the standards that it determines are valid. In a nutshell, the world dictates that your self-worth must be defined by any of the following attributes:

Money
Career
Education
Political power
Material wealth
Personal fitness
Outward Beauty
Popularity or fame
Personal achievement
Social media influence
Any "successes" derived from the above

Just look at our media-driven, socially accelerated, techno-linked world. Reality is what celebrities and the promoters of television and news shows say it is. People are emotionally connected to hundreds, if not thousands, or even millions of "followers" or "friends"—the vast majority of whom are complete strangers. Instant feedback for words and actions can leave a crushing wake of self-doubt and regret for those who make a seemingly innocent or carefree remark, caused solely by the sheer volume of negative responses elicited. Conversely, it can help support or reinforce the flimsiest of lies or valuations, regardless of how empty or unimportant those may be.

When all of that external pressure and oversight is layered on top of what we, as human beings already think about ourselves, it is no surprise that many of us (especially Christians) doubt who or what we are—whether we're even worthy or important enough to exist—much less to accomplish or achieve.

The emotional burdens of all that social media and tech nonsense is overwhelming. Add to that the fact that even professing Christianity in today's culture invites assault, making life even harder. Finally, when we link up those two treacherous components with our own unreasonable personal assessments and unfair self-perceptions, it's no wonder that so many of us Christians are easily lured, pulled away, or tempted to distance ourselves from the spiritual core values that God has placed within our beings.

(For the record, we're not suggesting that this is

acceptable or okay. We are only acknowledging that, for some, these are the causes or motivations behind certain behaviors and actions.)

So with all this external and internal pressure, the Christian often examines himself or herself, then asks some variant of the following questions:

"If I'm not good enough, or rich enough, or attractive enough, or smart enough, or *(fill in the blank)* enough. . . . and if I'm not happy with myself . . . how could God possibly be happy with me? **And why does it matter anyway?**"

To answer, let us begin with the very first man. God created Adam in His own image. It really doesn't matter if Adam was the "mirror image" of God, or if he just generally resembled God in form and shape. To think that the Creator of all things wanted his son (Luke 3:38) to look like Himself can only be described with our limited definition of pride. (Every proud father hopes to see himself in his sons and daughters.) He imbued Adam with power and authority similar to His own, to use over all the earth—enabling him to name all creatures and giving him dominion over everything (Genesis 2:19-20, Genesis 1:26), just as God Himself has dominion over all of creation.

Wow! That is quite an awesome responsibility. This surely doesn't sound like God wanted Adam to doubt himself, or doubt his place in the world. It shows that He wanted him to have the confidence and clear position of undeniable authority that He himself has. Someone who would question his own right to "be" could never fulfill God's directives. That is why it is imperative that we understand why our self-esteem is important to God. We cannot fulfill His plans for our lives if we never rise up beyond what we tend to think of ourselves. We cannot further His kingdom if we remain trapped in a darkened view of who and what we are.

Know this: it is not color, nor race, nor appearance, nor handicap, nor wealth, nor poverty, nor upbringing, nor age, nor anything else, internal or external that determines your value. God sees you as precious and prized, worthy of salvation through His Son, and worthy of His love and mercy. But He cannot force you to think that way about yourself. He can only give you the tools and the means for helping you to change your own mind. And God desires to see that change in you because, like Adam, He has a purpose for you. If you constantly beat yourself down—or allow others to do so—you will never feel the freedom of knowing that you have great value to Him. You are a pearl of great price (Matthew 13:46). It is only when we allow Him to free us from the measures and standards that a flawed and sinful world system has created, can we begin to fully enjoy and appreciate who we are . . . and most especially, who ***He*** is.

Let us emphasize this further. Many of us have often heard, "Even if you were the ***only*** one in all of human history who was willing to receive Jesus as Lord and Savior, He would have still carried out His plan to save you. He would have come to earth as a man, carried out his earthly ministry, and died just for you. He would have risen from the grave *just for you. That* is how much He loves you."

I believe this assertion to be truth, and I believe the Bible bears this out in so many ways. So I pose the question here, if the Father actually values each of us that much, do we inadvertently dishonor His intentions towards us by diminishing ourselves?

"For I know the thoughts I have towards you . . . thoughts of peace . . ." (Jeremiah 29:11)

Sidebar: It is critical at this point to emphasize that we are encouraging you to think of yourself as God thinks of you. This is not at all rooted in who or what you are. This is entirely based on who **He** is.

Paul said, *"A man should not think of himself more highly than he ought."* (Romans 12:3) Likewise, he also said *"But we will not boast of things without our measure . . ."* (II Corinthians 10:15) And further, *"But he that glorieth (or boasteth) let him glory (or boast) in the Lord."* (II Corinthians 10:17) These scriptures make it clearly evident that Paul was warning us to remain humble and not indulge in selfish and willful pride. Yet, he also understood his own place in, and his own relationship with, the Lord Jesus.
To state it another way, your sense of value, i.e., your self-esteem, should be solely attributed to how God

---

> sees you, what He desires for you, how He wants you to live, how He wants to help you live a fulfilling life, etc. You are extremely valuable because He has deemed you so. Nothing else, and no one else's opinion (even including your own), can compare to His assessment of your worth.

If we are now settled on the knowledge that God does indeed value us highly, then the next logical question to ask is not "Why?" but rather "Why is this so important to God?" It *is* important specifically because healthy self-esteem is critical to positive actions, behavior, and success. We all tend to have a brighter outlook and attitude when we feel good about ourselves and our lives. We are more interested, more motivated, and more determined to succeed when we feel optimistic. What you think about yourself will affect how others will perceive you. It will greatly impact your ability and opportunity to minister God's love to them, as well as their receptivity to your message.

People who always doubt themselves and lack any confidence or self-esteem can be an emotional drain on others. Their constant self-contempt and low self-worth seeps out into the lives of those around them, causing friends, family, and co-workers to eventually avoid them altogether. It is a slow poison that impedes positive words and actions from having any desirable or beneficial effect.

On the other hand, individuals who exude and express confidence are more likely to be motivated to achieve. They are positive thinkers with "can-do" attitudes, even when faced with life's challenges. They are also more resilient when dealing with personal setbacks. This is important because it is clear evidence to Believers and unbelievers alike—Christians with strong self-esteem believe God is on their side, and that He is ultimately in control of their lives. This is exactly why God wants us to have a generous amount of self-esteem—because He wants us to represent Christianity in such a way that sinners will see the joy and benefits of following Him. Then, they will feel compelled to meet Christ for themselves.

And that is fundamentally why our self-esteem is so important to God.

If our witness is secure, it is encouraging to unbelievers, and they will want to seek Him out. We can become the instruments of salvation for others to know Jesus. They will desire what we have. They will want their own personal relationships with God. And ultimately, that is what God wants. *"The Lord is . . . not willing that any should perish but that all should come to repentance."* (2 Peter 3:9)

It is _our_ surety, confidence, and joyfulness that will entice the unbeliever. But when we wallow in self-doubt and pity, when we allow the world to sift us as wheat, when we don't rely on His strength and His power, then we lose our effectiveness as His representatives. That makes it harder for God to use us for His glory. Elijah learned this in I Kings 19.

To lay the foundation here, we shall quickly review the chronology of Elijah's actions, and his state of mind prior to the events in Chapter 19.

- Chapter 17 of I Kings (v. 1) tells us how Elijah was instructed by God to tell King Ahab that there would be a drought until he (Elijah) said it was over. This drought was a direct result of Ahab's disobedience and provocations towards God. (Chapter 16: 30-33)
- 17:6 tells us that God arranged for ravens to bring Elijah bread and meat.
- In 17:13, Elijah directs the starving widow woman to make a meal for him first so that God can bless and save her and her son.
- Verses 17:19-22 explain how God raises the widow's dead son after Elijah's pleas.
- In 18:15, Elijah assures Obadiah that he will surely meet with King Ahab that very day.
- In verses 18:17-18, Elijah rejects Ahab's assertion that Israel is suffering because of him. Further, he calls Ahab out and blames him and his father for the problems of the day.
- In chapter 18:19-35, Elijah commands Ahab to gather all the prophets of Baal to come and participate in a test between God and Baal. He then sharply accuses Ahab of being double-minded about God, and throws down a challenge between Baal's prophets and himself—that fire sent from each "god" will

ignite their respective altar and sacrifice—with the true god prevailing over the other. Baal's prophets try and fail, as the prophet of God openly mocks them. Then Elijah purposefully makes it more challenging for himself by thoroughly soaking his altar and surrounding it in water.

- I Kings 18:35-39 says that a very confident Elijah prays openly to God, acknowledging Him as God, and himself as His prophet. Then, fire from heaven falls and consumes the altar and the water in the trench.
- Elijah instructs that Baal's prophets should all be rounded up, and taken to a place where he slays them all. I Kings 18:40
- Elijah orders King Ahab to eat quickly, and then head home because heavy rains are on the way.
- In verses 18:43-45, Elijah's prophecy comes true as the first rains in several years begin.

Stated plainly, these are not the words or deeds of a man who lacks *any* confidence in himself or his God. Elijah knew exactly how to proceed because he knew God was with him, directing him throughout. If Elijah had low self-esteem, he would not have been able to do all that God had planned. Instead, he saw himself as God saw him, and thus, he fulfilled his assignment and role as God's representative.

And yet . . .

This very same man—Elijah—who had publicly reprimanded the king of Israel, who ordered that same king (and others) around as if children, who openly mocked the false prophets and their god before the entire nation, who used his words and actions to proclaim God as God, and himself as His prophet, who killed four hundred and fifty false prophets, and who spoke rain into existence after a severe drought that he himself had declared three-plus years earlier—was so physically and spiritually exhausted and spent that he slid into self-pity, fear, and doubt. His self-esteem evaporated because Jezebel, Ahab's wife, vowed to kill him in retribution for what he had done. (I Kings 19:1-14) Most notably, in verse 4, Elijah asked God to end his life, comparing himself to his ancestors who had also failed God. All of Elijah's self-doubt and self-pity occurred *after* the amazing events we just described had transpired; and solely because one woman vowed to kill him.

Fortunately for Elijah, God wasn't joining in with any of his self-pity. He sent an angel to minister to him, and after a time, He gave instructions for further tasks in verses 15-21, including anointing a new king of Israel, and his own successor.

God sees the bigger picture. And He wants us to fulfill His plans for our lives in confidence and certainty of who He is, and by extension, who *we* are.

If Elijah had been granted his request to die, he would have never gone on to complete the many additional tasks and miracles that God had ordained for him to do.

So the most important point here is, God could not have used Elijah effectively if he was allowed to remain soaking in the toxins of low self-esteem. God wanted him out of that. He had more work for him to do. And the poisonous notions of "poor, pitiful me" were stalling God's plan. However, even at Elijah's lowest emotional point, God's valuation of him never changed nor wavered. Stated another way, God did not ever change His opinion of Elijah. It was Elijah who changed his opinion about himself. God sent His angel to help him overcome his low self-esteem, and eventually turn that around so he could once again see himself as God saw him.

In summary, self-esteem is critical to positive actions, behavior, and success. Without it, we doubt ourselves, we seek to escape from our responsibilities, and we seize up when it comes to doing things that need to be done. We _must_ have a healthy self-esteem to achieve. But as a Christian, your sense of self-value should be primarily derived from the value that God places on you. He always sees you at your best and most capable, regardless of how you see yourself—or how others see you. Therefore, let us rely entirely on God and the Lord Jesus to determine our own self-value. Let us rely on the instruction of the Holy Spirit to help us establish and maintain our self-worth.

Remember, *"For God so loved the world that He gave His only begotten Son, that whosever believeth on Him should not perish, but have everlasting life."*

That beautiful, lovely, and powerful verse has always included, and still does include, you.

3

GODLY SELF-ESTEEM VS. MAN'S SELF-ESTEEM

In our modern culture, it is not unusual for some people to gain fame and attention for some rather unimportant, and sometimes even insignificant reasons. Meanwhile, others become famous because of their talents and worldly accomplishments, as measured and determined by the world system of standards. These include musicians, actors and actresses, fashion models, etc. We do not dispute that these people may work hard or are skilled in their professions. But they are elevated to superstardom because of their ability to sing well, recite movie lines convincingly, or just plain look beautiful for a camera lens.

Then there are those who achieve and accomplish great things that society and culture recognize as important and significant. Sports stars, financial giants, inventors, and entrepreneurs are regarded highly for being the best or first in their chosen fields.

Creativity, hard work, and sometimes just plain luck converge to help these individuals make it to the peaks of their careers or industries.

Finally there are some who achieve fame through methods requiring no talent or real effort on their part. They may be an heir to a significant fortune or legacy, or they may have achieved infamy by questionable means and still managed to turn disgrace in their favor; subsequently acquiring celebrity status for previous unsavory behaviors, or less than honorable actions. The idea that they did something socially, legally, or morally unacceptable, and essentially "got away with it" (or got past it) is what often helps propel them to celebrity status.

Even among these aforementioned categories of personalities, there are varying degrees of talent, achievement, and notoriety that determine where they eventually rank among celebrity tiers and societal stations. So called "A-listers" are the hottest and most sought after individuals. They are the ones that everyone wants to be seen socializing alongside, and taking "selfies" with. "B-listers" and "C-listers" are constantly working to attend events to be seen with those people in the hopes of climbing higher up the celebrity strata. But the common goals for all are to be noticed and stay noticed. It is to see and be seen. It is to stay relevant and popular and desirable.

No doubt as we have briefly explored the celebrity universe here, you have recalled certain individuals who you see fitting into one or more of these categories. (In our technically advanced and instantaneously connected world, it would be quite an achievement for you to remain unaware of them and their star status.) These people derive a substantial amount of esteem and regard because of who they are, what they have done, or who their family is. But all that attention and idolization is rooted in the most shallow and unreliable of foundations—human emotions and admiration. This type of attention and reverence is fleeting, and can easily wane or be diverted away. Some celebrities may have "staying power", or an ability to remain in the public eye. But generally, as they age, marry and divorce, lose their youthful appearances, retire from their professions, etc., they are eventually supplanted by someone newer, younger, faster, better, more talented, or more interesting. Sadly, these fading stars often sink into deep depressions, alcohol and drug abuse, reclusiveness, and immoral entanglements. Without the crowds to distract them from themselves as well as artificially boost their self-esteem, these individuals are forced to examine their lives more closely, and they are often unhappy with who they really are. When self-esteem that is artificially created and sustained evaporates, then the individual is often left as a hollowed shell of their formerly glamorous self.

The self-esteem conferred and encouraged by man is briefly wonderful, but it is destined to crash and burn. It is derived from sources that rely heavily on the five natural senses. It is built upon rapidly passing moments of happiness, glory, and adulation.

By the way, a person need not be a famous celebrity

to fall victim to the same types of entrapments and snares resulting from artificially created self-worth. Family, friends, business associates, love interests, even acquaintances can temporarily contribute to your sense of self-esteem. But the fact is that it does not remain. Like celebrities, it must be consistently and constantly cultivated and nurtured. Otherwise, you can experience a sudden emotional drop that can be difficult to recover from, which can adversely impact you in every area of your life.

As Christians, we know that we have a sense of who we are, specifically because Jesus lives within us. He has given us an identity in Him. But although we are in this world, we should *"be not conformed to this world."* (Romans 12:1). However, events, people, and situations around us can cause us to shift attention away from the Lord and refocus it on ourselves. Once we have done this, it is all too easy to slip into a sort of deluded state where we have an artificially created and sustained assessment of personal self-esteem. We may become convinced, or even convince ourselves, that there is something very special and extraordinary about us. We begin to think that we are better, smarter, and more gifted than others. This euphoria of self may last for a time, but there is no doubt that it is doomed to failure. Fueling our self-images by temporary and human methods, which are often dependent on external factors not usually under our control, is a never ending task. Eventually and inevitably, this false self-esteem will run out or disappoint.

Sidebar: The Bible says to *"Humble yourselves therefore under the mighty hand of God, that He may exalt you in due time."* (I Peter 5:6) There is a very distinct line between receiving attention, honor, and adoration for ourselves as opposed to receiving it to honor God. The Lord wants you to be blessed and esteemed well, but He wants you to experience that specifically because He has made it possible; not you yourself, or as a result of those around you. Paul and Barnabas exemplified this when Paul healed a lame man at Lystra. The crowds were amazed and called them gods, but they vigorously admonished them by calling the people's attention to the one true God. (Acts 14:8-18).

There is an incredible example of Godly self-esteem versus human self-esteem found in the parable of the three servants and gold talents. For our purposes here, we shall focus on only that aspect of this parable. (This story is rich in God's wisdom and instruction, and we must urge you to study this passage more fully and completely so that you can derive even more understanding and guidance from the Holy Spirit.)

The parable is personally told by Jesus in Matthew 25:14-30. The main thrust of our analysis begins with *"And unto one he gave five talents, to another two, and to another one; to every man according to his several ability . . ."* (Matthew 25:15) Here, the master recognizes the actual abilities of each servant, gives each a measured amount of wealth, and then charges them with using their skills to increase his own fortune. The master knew these men, and esteemed these servants as able and capable.

For the first two men, it was _his_ assessment of their skills and knowledge that they each took personally with them as they worked on their assignment. As evidenced by their results, they performed precisely as he judged they would. They committed to their tasks, knowing that the master expected them to increase his money. They must have worked hard—and smart— to not only preserve the initial investment, but then to actually double their master's funds.

> <u>Sidebar</u>: There is one important and sometimes overlooked aspect of this story that we wish to spotlight. These servants most certainly saw and learned <u>how</u> to make money by watching their master as he conducted his own business affairs. They learned how to buy and sell, negotiate prices, control costs, and promote products. They likely spoke to familiar suppliers and customers, strategically evoking the name of their lord when it was wise and proper to do so. Whether their master was a seller of fine cloth, a tradesman, a farmer, or a rancher, these servants had been educated and well trained by the man they served. Likewise, the master had observed them enough to know what they were individually capable of—which helped him determine how many talents to entrust to each man. In short, the master did not "gamble" on these servants, just hoping they could produce a return. He had actually prepared them for this day, because he wanted to know if he would be

able to trust them with even more of his wealth and possessions. (Matthew 25: 21, 23)

The first two men did not regard themselves solely as servants. They did not discount what they had learned. Most importantly, they saw themselves as more than able to fulfill their master's directive because they took for themselves the image that their lord had of them—an image of a hard worker, one who makes smart decisions, and one who is able to get the task set before him done. This is what drove them on to success.

The third servant did not see himself as his master saw him. Instead, he paid more attention to his own self-image and self-esteem—*his human self-esteem*—to the point that he was paralyzed and ineffective. He did not do as he was trained. He made a poor and lazy decision in doing nothing. He did not like the fact that the master would benefit from _his_ hard work. So he foolishly planned, expecting to give back to his lord the exact same measure of gold that he had started with. The end result was that no one benefitted from this man's selfish and self-centered focus—least of all, the servant himself.

How much more could we do if we would allow ourselves to see what God sees in each of us? If we took the instruction and training and guidance of our Lord, emboldened by His view of us, what could we accomplish for His kingdom and in His name?

As we continue to consider Godly self-esteem compared to human self-esteem, we should be mindful of the following scriptures.

"All our righteousnesses are as filthy rags." (Isaiah 64:6)
"O Lord . . . we are the clay, and thou our potter; and we all are the work of thy hand." (Isaiah 64:8)

It is not wise to invest our ego and self-worth in the assessments of mere men or women. The absolute and very best that they can give us is worth nothing before the Lord God. Further, if we are all clay, as noted in Isaiah 64:8, then what benefit is there to being admired and revered by other lumps of clay? Does one piece of clay have superior stature or standing, enabling it to overvalue or undervalue another? Definitely not. It is the potter who decides worth; not the other pieces of clay. Furthermore, not even an individual piece of clay has the right or authority to rate itself. We would all do well in remembering this.

Sidebar: We have a saying which was originated by the author's earthly father. It is somewhat based on Acts 10:34 where it says clearly that *"God is no respecter of persons."* This essentially means that He sees us all as redeemable, and worthy of His time and attention—as much as He has these for anyone else.

The saying goes, "God sees us all the same. You are not better than anyone else; but no one else is better than you." Certainly, God recognizes us all as different—that is how He intentionally created us. But the real message in this saying is that not a single one of us has any superior standing or position over another. Celebrity or not, professional or not, educated or not, white or black, male or female, and so on; God neither respects nor regards us any more highly than another. Jesus made the same sacrifice for all. God's blessings are available for all. And as we have stated already, God would have put into motion His entire plan of salvation—if only to rescue you alone.

We must realize that the sayings or judgments of men have little to do with our true worth. The standards and constructs of society can never at all accurately measure our true value. There is no amount of fandom, glamour, media attention, financial or political power, or worldly achievements that can even come close to how God sees and values us. In the final analysis, His esteem for us is all that really and truly matters.

4

GOD'S GENEROUS SUPPLY OF SELF-ESTEEM FOR YOU

Just moments before, I had gotten another all too familiar phone call.

"I'm sorry, Mr. Jones is going to have to cancel his follow-up appointment with you today," the secretary's voice said.

"Okay. Shall we reschedule our meeting for later this week?" I asked.

"Uh, no. He asked me to tell you that he's reconsidered your product and decided it's not right for us at this time. But he'll keep your information on file and if anything changes, he'll give you a call back."

In my selling experience, this was the kiss-off of death. I had just been exiled to the island of "if anything changes," a place where failed sales reps are sent, to be tormented by the specters of past sales rejections. (A little melodramatic, I know.)

What made this even harder was the fact that the product being rejected was one I had developed myself. I was emotionally and financially invested in it. I had devoted incredible hours and spent my limited resources in developing a prototype and sales brochures. I felt like I had a winning product and a polished presentation. I had years of quality training and excellent sales experience. And, most importantly—I really, truly, and *honestly* believed that God had given me the whole idea, and had selected me to carry it out. How could it not succeed?

But this was my third cancellation in a week which already followed several weeks of numerous cancellations and <u>no</u> sales. If I'd had dozens of appointments lined up and had already experienced some sales success, I would have kept rolling along. But cold-calling strangers is tough. Especially when you want to sell them a product that has never been seen before. There is no history of success you can point to. The whole concept is untested, unfamiliar, and unknown. The customers' often-asked questions are basically, "What are you selling?" and "Why do we need to meet?" Their often-used responses are "Let's see what others do with it," and "Maybe we'll try it later." I did succeed in that I was able to get many first-time appointments. But it was the follow-up meetings, meant to close the sale, which were drying up and evaporating into thin air.

Now, I must say that I've developed a pretty tough hide over the years. I have been rejected by the best and brightest, as well as the most selfish and incompetent, of potential customers. But I have to be honest, there's only so much rejection a person can take, even in a profession where you can expect that the customer's first line of defense will always be "No thanks. I'm not interested."

I was really starting to feel pretty low. My self-esteem was shot to pieces. And it was getting harder and harder to pick myself up each day and keep moving forward when the possible rewards just seemed to move farther and farther away. I started to seriously ponder and question myself in so many ways.

"Maybe I'm not cut out for sales." *(Really? After years of countless successes and multiple sales awards with several Fortune 50 companies?)*

"Maybe I'm not doing this right." *(After all, it is a new product, and there will be a learning curve to promoting it properly.)*

"Maybe God picked the wrong guy." *(That's what this is really all about, isn't it?)*

I was feeling really sorry for myself, and I wanted God to know about it. Remember our discussion about Elijah in a previous chapter? Well, unlike Elijah, my life wasn't in danger, and I wasn't ready to ask God to let me die—but I did feel so down on myself, that I was ready to give up on the whole thing.

After the phone call ended, I decided I would go ahead and finish getting ready. I had no other appointments for the day, the rest of the week, or even the week following. But I had already showered, ironed my clothes, and was just about to shave when I got the cancellation call. Fighting back tears, (yes, tears) I lathered up my face with shaving cream and proceeded to have a one-sided conversation with God.

"Lord, I really believed that this idea was from you. I thought I was giving it my best. I thought that customers were going to jump all over this opportunity. And yet, nothing is happening. I'm just getting beat up out there. Everyone says I have a great idea, but no one is willing to put their dollars on the table for it. Without sales, I'm just wasting my time. I feel like a fool. And I know you don't mess up, so it must be me. I'm missing something here. Maybe my heart isn't in the right place. Maybe I'm not as good as I thought I was. *I really don't know why You picked me to do this, if You knew I was going to fail.*"

I have had several instances in my life where the Lord speaks up so clearly inside of me, and in such a powerful way, that there is no doubt it is Him. This was one of those times.

"Frank, I knew who you were when I called you. And I also know what you're capable of becoming."

Well, how's that for a lightning bolt of revelation?

I stopped mid-shave and looked at myself in the mirror as I wept. God had cared enough to speak to me personally about my struggle. He subtly acknowledged my efforts and assured me that He hadn't lost faith in me, even when I had lost faith in myself. Then He reminded me of what I had learned years earlier in church:

"Don't confuse the journey with the destination."

At that moment, I felt God release me from that project. Although I would have liked to see it bear fruit in terms of financial success, that was never what it was about for God. He'd always known about my weaknesses and shortcomings. He wasn't as impressed as I was with my past successes either. He wanted me to be obedient. He wanted me to put forth the effort. He wanted me to learn and mature and grow. In my case, He didn't care about sales projections, high-level meetings with company presidents, or financial rewards. He cared about <u>me</u>. It was always about me. Not because of who I am, but because of who He is, and who He wants me to be.

More than that, He implied that better things were to come when He spoke about me in the future tense. That was confirmation that great things awaited. I don't know what and I don't know when, but they are definitely out there. I just need to stick with God and find out about them as He reveals them to me.

Like Elijah, I gave up on myself. But God has never given up on me. And He'll never give up on you either. He has provided for your self-esteem as much as He has for any other area of your life. If you believe that *"no good thing will He withhold from them that walk uprightly"* (Psalms 84:11), then you must also believe that your sense of self-worth is part of that. He doesn't want your spirit crushed, your hope shattered, and your self-esteem destroyed. How could that possibly serve Him? How could you effectively work for Him if you are so emotionally scarred and battered? No, He wants you to be strong in Him. *"Be strong in the Lord and the power of His might."* (Ephesians 6:10). He wants you to have hope in Him. *"Now the God of hope fill you with all joy and peace in believing, that ye may abound in hope, through the power of the Holy Ghost."* (Romans 15:13). He wants you to have peace in Him. *"The peace of God, which passeth all understanding, shall keep your hearts and minds through Christ Jesus."* (Philippians 4:7).

God has provided a generous, abundant, more-than-enough supply of self-esteem for you to draw from. And the following scripture will help you begin the process which will set your mind free—if you will just receive it—and allow the Holy Spirit to build on this truth in your life. To get started, understand that this next verse is a never ending well of cleansing water, meant for your mental and emotional restoration. It is evertrue. It always fits your situation.

It will never run out, or run dry, or expire. It is how God saw you yesterday. It is how He will see you tomorrow. It is how He sees you <u>at this very moment</u>.

"There is therefore now no condemnation to them that are in Christ Jesus, who walk not after the flesh, but after the Spirit." (Romans 8:1)

Tell me, when is *now*? That's right. *Now* is this very moment—this present time. But in a few hours, at that time, it will also be *now*. And exactly forty-eight hours ago, at that moment, <u>that</u> was *now*. No matter what point in time we choose on the calendar—past, present, or future—for any specific or particular moment—*in that moment*—it will always be *now*. It was *now* when Paul wrote this verse two thousand years ago. It was *now* when you were saved. It was *now* when you purposely, willfully, or selfishly, sinned again. It will be *now* before <u>and</u> after you ask God to forgive you for messing up.

What's more, it was *now* <u>every time</u> you felt bad about yourself; when you felt unloved, or ugly, or overweight, or inadequate, or broke, or sick, or anything else that has come your way. But there was no condemnation for you then. There is no condemnation for you *now*. And while you, others, or the enemy may try to convince you of your unworthiness, God doesn't project those "vibes" towards you. His inclinations are thoughts of peace, and love, and redemption. *"For I know the thoughts I have towards you . . . thoughts of peace . . ."* (Jeremiah 29:11)

So, in Romans 8:1 alone, God makes it absolutely and irrefutably clear how He regards you. He does not see you as a failure. He does not see you as a fraud—pretending to be a Christian when you are not. He doesn't see an unattractive, undesirable, ignorant, foolish, poverty-stricken loser. He _only_ sees you as His own; someone He has set free through His Son, Jesus. And He sees you that way **_right now!_**

Sidebar: We are instructed to walk "after the Spirit." God clearly doesn't want us to sin. It distresses Him when we do. But He has made provision through Christ to absolve us of all our sins. If you have sinned, or are engaging in sinful behavior, **GO DIRECTLY TO JESUS!** _"And if any man sin, we have an advocate with the Father, Jesus Christ the righteous."_ (I John 2:1) Confess your sins, repent (turn your mind, attitude, heart) to God, seek forgiveness, and then ask the Holy Spirit to deliver you from whatever the root causes of those behaviors might be. Then as quickly as you can, get back into a solid and firm relationship with the Father. Remember, He knew about your sin the moment you committed it. You can't hide from Him what He already knows. Ask for forgiveness immediately, and then move on. There is no condemnation any more from God. And if the Creator won't condemn you, then by what right does anything, or anyone (including yourself), have to dangle that sin in your face? Don't ever again let that get in the way of your relationship with the Lord.

The Bible is full of indicators that God has, among

all of His blessings, a never-ending supply of what you'll need to have good self-esteem. Bear in mind that these verses are not necessarily stand-alone or totally singular in their importance. But together, they will help you form a rock solid, interlocking foundation of how God sees you. They will firmly and solidly establish in your heart and mind that the enemy's lies, temptations, and tauntings are nothing more than empty allegations paired with raucous bullying. And it doesn't matter if such accusations are internal or from some external source either. Whether it be a friend or foe, family or co-worker, social media or self-scrutiny—*if it runs contrary to what God says about you, it's false and only deserves the time and effort necessary to take authority over it in Jesus' name.*

Let us now confirm with further evidence that God sees you differently than how others may see you, or how you see yourself:

"But be of good cheer. I have overcome the world." (John 16:33)
"We are more than conquerors through Him that loved us." (Romans 8:37)

Jesus Himself tells us in the first verse that we should take joy in the knowledge that He has overcome all the sin and darkness the world can muster. His statement is intended to be all-inclusive. There is nothing that the world can throw at Him that He has not taken Lordship over. *"And Jesus came and spake unto them, saying, All power is given unto me in heaven and in earth."* (Matthew 28:18) Even death could not defeat the Lord. He said that <u>*only He*</u> had the power to lay down His life, and then to take it up again. (John 10: 17-18)

When you couple the second verse with the first, you have a spiritual one-two combination punch that is unbeatable. We are <u>more</u> than conquerors through Him. *Him who?* The same Him who overcame the world—***Jesus***. Jesus is in your corner. He's there to help you get through the fight. And He's not only encouraging you and coaching you, He's telling you that your enemy is already beaten, because He beat him first. What's more, and this is the really good part, Jesus has **confidence** in you. If God the Son, Creator of all that is, believes in you, how is it that you can even begin to doubt yourself? Why would you ever let anyone's words, or your own physical appearance, or your failures or unfulfilled dreams, dictate whether or not you are an overcomer and a conqueror? He has already said of Himself that He is both, and because you are in Him, you are as well.

*"Herein is our love made perfect . . . because as He **is**, so are we in this world."* (I John 4:17)

"As He is, so are we" speaks of the present tense, i.e., <u>right now</u>. As we've said, *now* means <u>this very moment in time</u>. So with that as our framework, let's ask a few specific and direct questions.

Is Jesus sick . . . *now?*
Is He broke . . . *now?*
Is He uncertain about His position . . . *now?*
Does He question His own authority . . . *now?*
Does Jesus think that He's not good enough . . . *now?*
Does He doubt His relationship with God the Father . . . *now?*

The singular answer to all these questions, and any others like them, is a loud, forceful, and resounding ***NO!***

<u>Sidebar</u>: You might be thinking, "All of this is good. I get it. Jesus is great. He's God of everything. But that's just it . . . He's GOD. I'm just me. I fail sometimes. I make mistakes. I sin when I know it's wrong or even when I try not to. I'm not happy with my appearance. I have physical problems or health issues. I'm not as friendly or well-liked as others. I still can't figure out what to do with my life. My past is too dark. I have too many personal issues". And on . . . and on . . . and on. Well, dear brother and sister in Christ, welcome to the human race. I personally believe that one of the devil's most successful and widespread campaigns against Believers is promoting the lie where we tend to think that we are the only person who struggles with these types of problems and thoughts. But here's the real truth: Not everyone has everything in common, but the entire human race has common experiences. There is not a single culture that doesn't have people, who at some point, fail, or doubt, or sin, or disbelieve, or act

---

greedy, or get angry, or act selfishly, etc. And all of them . . . and all of us . . . and **you**, are exactly the persons Jesus came to redeem and restore.

It's time we stop basing our sense of self-value and self-worth on what we do, how we are, or what we think. ***We need to focus our self-esteem on who He is, what He's done, what He has, and where He is.*** These scriptures, among others, clearly and definitively state or imply that we are to draw our value from <u>Him</u>. He is King of kings, Lord of lords, and Overcomer of the world. We are worthy because He made us that way. We are God's children because we were adopted into His family. We are heirs and joint-heirs with Jesus!

Pray this confession aloud right now:

Lord Jesus, thank You for all You have done. Thank You for delivering me from all manner of bondage, including self-doubt, and low self-esteem.

Lord Jesus, if there are any sins, in words or deeds that I have committed against You, I ask for Your forgiveness. Cleanse me from all unrighteousness and restore me to a position of right-standing with the Father. Thank You Jesus, for being my Mediator and Advocate.

From this moment forward, I confess and I profess that I am the righteousness of God in Christ Jesus. I proclaim and decree that according to God's Word, I am an overcomer in Him. I am a conqueror through Him. I will not regard what the world says about me. I will only confess what God says about me. I am the head and not the tail. I am blessed going in, and blessed coming out. I am above only, and not beneath. I am blessed in the city and in the country.

Lord, I want to be and do everything You want for me. I accept how You see me. I reject every action, every word, and every thought that tries to diminish who I am in You. I am who You say I am, and I am that <u>because</u> of You.

Thank you for renewing my mind and my heart to reflect Your love and power in my life. In Your name I pray and confess these things. Amen.

Repeat this confession and prayer once a day, twice per day, or as often as needed. Study the scriptures on which it is based. Meditate on the meanings behind the words. Be assured that every time you do, you are allowing the Holy Spirit to work positive changes in your life. And each time, you will be reminding yourself that He is the provider of your worth and self-esteem. Take comfort and assurance in the knowledge that the enemy is being forced to release his grip on your opinions about yourself. You are not required to build up and maintain your own self-esteem. Your goal is to develop your understanding of how God esteems you. Once you fully recognize that God prizes you highly and values you greatly, your self-esteem will follow. Again, not because of who <u>you</u> are, *but because of who He is.*

Need further confirmation of your great worth and value to God? Then let's analyze the following scripture passages.

"God, who is rich in mercy, because of His great love . . . made us alive together with Christ . . . and raised us up together, and made us to sit together in . . . Christ Jesus." (Ephesians 2:4-6)
"We are His workmanship . . . created in Christ Jesus." (Ephesians 2:10)

God's abundant mercy and love are the basis for what follows. But first, consider that God has extended His love and mercy to us all. Why? Because we are valuable to Him. He offers these things to us merely because He chooses to. There is nothing that requires God to extend any mercy or love at all towards us. We certainly haven't earned them, nor can we ever deserve them. They are outright gifts. And just what are the effects of those gifts? The end results are that God has made us alive together, raised us together, and allowed us to sit together with, and created in, Christ Jesus. And where is Jesus? He is at the right hand of God. (Hebrews 10:12) This is a place of the highest and greatest honor. We are now partakers of His table, members of His entourage, and part of His inner circle.

Once again, I pose the important question—if God now esteems you so highly because of your present affiliation with Jesus—then what creature, what thought, what temptation, what behavior, or what entity exists—whether natural or supernatural, real or imagined—that can assault your right to see yourself as God sees you?

There is an old axiom among Christian circles: "Be patient, God isn't finished with me yet." There is a substantial amount of truth to this saying. Unfortunately, more often than not, we have used it as a rationale, or a defensive method, for deflecting away criticism for our own shortcomings and failures. By employing this motto in that way, we are not only excusing ourselves from being all that Christ desires for us, but we are also inadvertently and unintentionally dwelling on our mistakes and flaws. It is God's intention that we become more Christ-like as we journey through our Christian walk. It is not His desire that we remain shackled to the sins, behaviors, or ideas that He delivered us from in the first place.

"We are His workmanship . . . created in Christ Jesus," tells us two very important things of which we should always be mindful.

1. First, God has a plan for developing and growing us to be what He wants us to be. *"The steps of a good man are ordered by the Lord, and He delighteth in his way."* (Psalm 37:23) Does this not speak volumes about what He thinks of us and that we are important to Him? Why would the Creator of all there is, even bother with any one of us? *It's because He loves us.*
2. Second, we are created in Christ Jesus. *"If any man be in Christ, he is a new creature:* **old things are passed away; behold, all things are**

become new." (II Corinthians 5:17) Well, what do you think about that? I do believe that God has made a way for us to escape not only eternal damnation, but also the former life of sins, afflictions, addictions, shame, etc. that we came from. Once more, *He did it solely because He loves us.*

He is loving. He is generous. He is forgiving. He is merciful. He is kind. His ability to raise us up from the muck and mire of sin, self-destruction, and self-pity knows no limits. But why? Why does He do this? What does God possibly have to gain from it? How does He personally benefit from extending such boundless grace to a group of creatures who seem bent on keeping their distances from One so full of love? For we are the ones who push Him away by virtue of our sins, behaviors, words, attitudes, and deeds. And yet, *"If we confess our sins, he is faithful and just to forgive us our sins, and to cleanse us from all unrighteousness."* (I John 1:9).

The answers defy what we have long believed, and even how we think. For we cannot define God and measure Him against what we know, or what we perceive. He is so much greater than that. We cannot project our own ideas, or attribute our own motivations to anything He has done, or will ever do. In short, you can't fit a huge mountain into a small ditch. And you can't define anything that God does by the notions and goals of our imperfect and flawed human leanings and understandings.

"For my thoughts are not your thoughts, neither are your ways my ways, saith the LORD." (Isaiah 55:8).

The answer can be found in a significant verse that we already noted earlier.

*"For God so loved the world that **He gave** . . ."* (John 3:16)

So when some ask, "Why would God do what He did? Why would Jesus go through so much trouble and pain to die for my sins?" The answer is right here in this verse. Yes, He loved the world so very much. But equally important, and no less conspicuous, is the fact that *"He gave"*. God is a *giver*. He delights in giving. He enjoys it. It pleases Him. It makes Him happy. It drives His actions and decisions. *"No good thing will He withhold from them that walk uprightly."* (Psalms 84:11)

Sidebar: God wants us to experience life abundantly. But take heed. He is not a fairy godmother who exists only to grant magical wishes. He is not a genie who stands ready to be commanded; to fulfill whatever biddings you may request. He desires to bless us, but He does so as part of His plan for our lives. He is not interested in indulging our lusts or our selfish interests. He searches out our thoughts and intents as a pre-requisite to blessing us. He wants us to have what we ask; so long as it is not contrary to His Word, or rooted strictly in personal gain, covetousness, or idolatry.

> I recommend that you explore God's Word and seek His insight in a greater and more meaningful way, as this important topic merits more extensive personal study.

So then, we once again firmly establish God's wonderful intentions towards us. His purposes are honorable, pure, and indisputable. It is now our job to allow ourselves to be persuaded of these things. His giving towards us is <u>intentional</u>, and meant to save us; to raise us up; to deliver us; to provide for us; to heal us; to guide us; and so much more. Once we become convinced that God has the best for us, and desires the best for us, then it becomes easier to realize that He is on our side.

"If God be for us, who can be against us?" (Romans 8:31)

We must come to an understanding that He is on our side. If we can internalize and grab hold of this truth, then every future battle, temptation, sinful downfall, and personal shortcoming cannot diminish or destroy our standing with Him. We have a place of righteousness with Him that He has provided for us. He *gave* us that position. We are there because of Him, and <u>only</u> because of Him. But we are there nonetheless. As we said earlier of the Prodigal son, even in the midst of all his debauchery and sin, he never ceased to be the son of his father. That blood relationship was established *forever.* Thankfully, he eventually came to his senses and went home to seek his father's forgiveness. The man saw his son from afar, and he knew why he had returned. The father embraced and loved him as he always had, and did not hesitate for a moment to restore his lost son to a rightful place in his house. Unworthy as the son felt, the father still esteemed him so highly that he immediately ordered a feast in his son's honor. I imagine that the son wept openly as he finally realized that he had always had great value—not because of money or so-called friends, but because his father loved him unconditionally and regarded him as precious. It was the father who imparted to his son a sense of self-worth. No doubt the son humbly and gratefully received his father's gifts of forgiveness and restoration, since there is no mention that the spontaneous feast, to be held in the son's honor, was cancelled.

So it is with you and God the Father. You have a place of honor in His house, regardless of your behavior or sin. And unworthy as you may feel, He conveys to you His sense of your personal value. *You are not just "worth something" to God, you are "worth everything" to Him.* He celebrates your return, and He is anxious for you to resume your rightful place and position in His house.

So then, if God so truly and deeply loves us, if we are His "pearls of great price", how then can we continue to hold on to our own beliefs that we have little or no value? Is this idea not rooted in nothing more than our own lack of understanding Him, and our limited knowledge of the tremendous breadth and unlimited depth of His love?

You are not just *worth something* to God, you are **worth everything** to Him.

It is time we turn our backs on the long held doctrines that insinuate we are lowly creatures in God's sight. It is time we reject the long history of so called faith that tells us that we are nobodies who are just lucky enough to barely get saved and hobble into the Lord's kingdom. The time is now to fully embrace the true relationships we are to have with God the Father. *We* are the prodigals. Yes, we have wandered away from our Father's house, searching for love and belonging. We have taken the blessings of our Father and squandered them on selfish and youthful lusts. We have reached our own personal low points and realized that we are nothing without our Father. And we have no self-esteem because we are nothing—we have nothing—without Him.

Let us return to our Father's house. Let Him restore us to a position of right-standing with Him. Let Him honor us because He sees us as precious. Though we are undeserving, let Him **give** us a robe, a ring, and a feast because it pleases Him to do so. Let us humbly and deliberately acknowledge that He has given us worth . . . that we have self-value and self-esteem because He has provided it to us. We are valuable and treasured because He has declared us to be. And He has manifested that through His repeated acceptance of us, even with all our imperfections and quirks, and regardless of how much, or how often, we fail.

Finally, we must turn away from those influences that seek to pull us back into the quagmires of lust, self-pity, sin, and self-devaluation. It is virtually impossible for one to *"keep your heart with all diligence"* (Proverbs 4:23) if you are constantly and repeatedly exposing yourself to the very same factors that have successfully dragged you down before. The sources of negativity that consistently led to the destruction of your self-esteem will not join your personal quest to change how you think about yourself. Whether friend, family, or co-worker; music, movies, or social media; fashion trends or social circles; the influences that continue to attempt to infuse you with detrimental ideas and images will not cease on their own. They have no reason nor any incentive to stop. It is therefore incumbent on you to seek out replacements for them that will reinforce the message that God is for you, not against you. Instead of dwelling on, or flirting with, the spiritually unhealthy, follow the instructions Paul has given us: *"Finally, brethren, whatsoever things are true, whatsoever things are honest, whatsoever things are just, whatsoever things are pure, whatsoever things are lovely, whatsoever things are of good report; if there be any virtue, and if there be any praise, think on these things."* (Philippians 4:8) As you abandon those things which can only corrupt, you will come to rely more and more on the Holy Spirit for strength and determination. As time passes, those negative influences will begin to lose their appeal—they will diminish in their strength to persuade you. Their ability to entice you will begin to wane. You will be stronger and more prepared to resist the thoughts and temptations which once held you captive. Most of all, you will certainly know that your freedom from all manner of sin and affliction, including the affliction of low self-esteem, comes from the Lord—because He has provided it for you. You will begin to think, act, and live out, the overcoming life that He has willed for you in His Word.

5

PUTTING GODLY SELF-ESTEEM INTO ACTION

How shall we put our Godly self-esteem to work in our lives? Self-esteem has no tangible mass that can be measured or weighed. It has no volume, and cannot be held in the palm of your hand to be handled or manipulated. You can't just take a dab of it and smooth over facial lines and wrinkles. Or swallow a capsule of it to boost your self-confidence or energy level.

The application of God's self-esteem for you comes through your consistent use of the knowledge of God's Word. You must memorize, internalize, finalize (in your thinking), and _verbalize_ scriptures like the ones we have referenced thus far. You should remind yourself daily, or even multiple times a day, that you are worthy and remarkable because He has deemed you to be.

As you walk in this newfound freedom, as you practice and live out the knowledge that you are redeemed from the curse of self-devaluation, then you will be more able to yield to the direction and guidance of the Holy Spirit. You will be more ready and available for God to direct your paths and enhance your destiny in Him. You will become a more capable minister of Jesus' love and grace. You will speak with the confidence and assurance that what God desires for you is the very best of what He has to offer.

Sidebar: It would serve us well to remember that God does not have a "one-track mind" nor is He a "one-trick pony". This book is about God and your self-esteem, but that is not the only aspect about you that He cares about, nor is it the only characteristic important to Him. Do not allow yourself to be deceived into just believing that "God says I'm okay, so therefore everything else will be okay. I'll just keep rolling along and stop every once in a while to offer a kind word, or perform a good deed." As Believers, we are tasked with the responsibility to become intimate with His complete message of redemption. This includes, but is not limited to, salvation, forgiveness, mercy, grace, love, worship, thankfulness, healing, deliverance, faith, etc. It is imperative that we pursue the fullness of God, so that we can always be ready to minister His wonderful gifts to anyone in need.

So, to initiate the study of how to put your Godly self-esteem into action, we shall examine several examples that the Bible makes available to us. With the exception of our first example—Jesus, and His life here on earth—we will review how various individuals in the Bible fared before embracing God's gift of self-esteem, as well as how they did afterwards. But there are two critical things to remember as we progress through these profiles:

1. This is not an all-inclusive list—either in numbers of individuals, or experiences they had.
2. All of these individuals (except for the Lord Jesus) are regular people who are made of the same stuff as you and I—born of flesh and predisposed to sin. They faced troubles, trials, and temptations as we do today. They were as flawed and uncertain as we are. The key point to remember here is this: You and I can take our own difficulties and challenges and overlay our experiences over theirs. There are enough similarities to make the comparisons meaningful. We may not fear for our lives as Elijah once did, or face being shipwrecked like Paul, but we have faced enough adversities to validate what we can learn from them.

The Self-Esteem of Jesus

Without question, Jesus is the most exceptional human who ever lived. Yet the Bible also tells us that He was the only begotten Son of God. Naturally, we can surmise that would carry with it a high degree of self-assurance, self-confidence, and self-esteem. But while Jesus had a clear sense of who He was, while living His life here on earth, He had to contend with everything the entire human race has had to face. *"For we have not an high priest which cannot be touched with the feeling of our infirmities; but was in all points tempted like as we are, yet without sin."* (Hebrews 4:15). This is the main reason we will examine His life first. For it is His earthly life and conduct to which we should aspire. He was the personification of how a follower could walk and live on this earth.

The first instance that draws our attention is when twelve year old Jesus is found to have remained behind in the temple at the end of his parents' pilgrimage. He acts surprised that His earthly parents would not have already known or realized that He *"must be about His Father's business."* (Luke 2:49) The teachers and elders speaking with Jesus also marveled at His level of understanding and knowledge. It becomes obvious that Jesus had a distinct and very certain sense of self and purpose—at twelve years old! How wonderful would it be for us have that same clarity in our lives, regardless of our ages. The confidence Jesus showed at such a young age is evidence that He was putting His self-esteem on the line, so to speak, without hesitation or reservation.

The next incident that conveys Jesus' personal conviction about His own self-worth is when He goes to the river Jordan to be baptized by John the Baptist.

John was astonished that Jesus was seeking to be baptized by him, when in fact he felt Jesus should be the baptizer. (Matthew 3:13-17) But John is instructed by Jesus to proceed, knowing this action is all part of God's plan for man's redemption. To cap off the event, the Holy Spirit in the form of a dove descends upon Jesus, **and then** there is a voice from heaven that says, *"This is my beloved Son, in whom I am well pleased."* These are defining events where Jesus has put His self-worth into action. They not only clarify who He is, but they are the result of His acting on His own self-value. No one else in history can even come close to the self-confidence Jesus had about who He was. And yet, what is even more amazing, is the fact that He desires that we should be like Him. (*"He that saith he abideth in Him, ought himself also to walk, even as He walked."* (I John 2:6))

Now consider for a moment how you would regard yourself if the following things had happened to you:

1. The greatest Abrahamic covenant prophet—John—publicly declares you to be the one to take away the sins of the world (John 1:29).
2. You are baptized by this same prophet, after he expresses his reverence and deference to you. (Matthew 3:14)
3. The Holy Spirit of God descends upon you in the form of a dove. Particularly in biblical times, this most certainly would be regarded as a visible sign from God Himself. (Matthew 3:16)

4. A loud and unseen voice from the heavens proclaims you to be God's beloved Son. (Matthew 3:17)

Initially, we might think that these events would bolster anyone's confidence and self-esteem. And who in their right mind could argue that there was nothing distinctive about Jesus after having witnessed such amazing and wonderful things? Even more, if these events had happened to any one of us, they would certainly help to persuade us that we are something special. We would derive a tremendous boost of self-worth and self-confidence from having experienced these events. But . . . that is exactly how *we* think—that is not at all how *God* thinks.

Jesus already **knew** who He was. Let me reiterate: Jesus—*God, the Son*—knew *exactly* who He was *before* He ever approached John the Baptist. He was merely participating in the Father's plan of redemption as He should. He was not impressed that the greatest Old Testament prophet recognized Him. He had no reservations in telling John to baptize Him as instructed by God, the Father. He was not surprised that the Holy Spirit, in the form of a dove, flew down onto Him. And He was not amazed, shocked, or frightened that a disembodied voice from heaven confirmed aloud for all present to hear, that He was God's own Son. ***That*** is how Jesus put His own self-esteem into action. He was self-assured, and He acted upon what He knew to be true. His confidence was not derived from what transpired at the Jordan River.

His confidence in Himself and God beforehand is what enabled Him to speak and behave as He did. In other words, His self-assurance prompted Him to act in this manner. He wasn't confident *because* of what happened—He was already confident, and that's _why_ these things happened.

Another example of Jesus' self-assurance is found in Mark 5:35-43. Here, He is besought by a worried father, Jairus, whose daughter is sick and near death. Jesus is literally on the way to the man's house when someone comes to tell them that it is too late. He turns to Jairus and says, *"Do not be afraid; only believe."* Jesus walked into the house, where those present were weeping loudly and wailing, and asked them why they were making such a commotion over the child's death. He said that she was not dead, but only sleeping.

Apparently, the mourners were quickly able to turn their loud cries of supposed grief into scornful laughter (which makes us wonder just how genuine all their sorrow actually was in the first place). Undeterred by their behavior and reactions, Jesus sent them all out, then accompanied the father and mother into the child's room. He took her by the hand, told her to "arise", and she got up and walked. Clearly, and once again, Jesus was sure in Himself and His Father, as He proceeded to minister to a family in great need. He took that self-assurance and put it into action as He raised that girl from the dead. He had no doubts about Himself, or what He was about to do. He was confident and comfortable in His own skin, and the taunting and ridiculing of those nearby had no bearing on who He was, or His ability and willingness to minister life to a dead child.

If you or I had just performed such a miracle, it is very likely that we would have beamed over what had just occurred and the fact that God used us in such a wonderful way. As the news of our actions spread, we would probably begin to feel a sense of accomplishment and importance over what we did. Truly, God did the miracle, but the very fact that He used <u>us</u> to bring it about would immediately increase our own sense of worthiness and self-esteem. In short, we would probably be wearing a mile-wide grin and feeling quite thrilled with our participation, as well as the final results.

But Jesus acted in exactly the opposite manner. He instructed the parents to remain quiet about the whole thing. This is evidence that He didn't want (or need) the attention and adulation that would most certainly result from the news of this miracle. Jesus was sure of Himself before the event; and He was still sure of Himself afterwards. His self-esteem was present and more than sufficient the whole time. And it was completely unaffected by the outcome. Although we're not exactly sure why He told the parents to keep quiet about what transpired, the larger point is that He neither desired nor required the inevitable chatter of the crowds to reinforce His sense of self-worth and position. He didn't need to hear the masses say He was sent by God . . . He already knew He was.

Sidebar: We could further examine why Jesus told the parents to stay quiet. Unfortunately, that would take us too far off the main theme of this book, so we shall not pursue it. But we would like to posit that the parents remaining silent was almost a complete impossibility anyway. The "mourners" who were witnesses to the daughter's death most certainly learned of her restoration. They would seek out answers and explanations. They would talk amongst themselves. In addition, Jairus was a ruler of the synagogue. It is not likely that his high-profile profession would allow him to remain inconspicuously quiet—even if he had purposed in himself to do so. Finally, from a strictly personal perspective, if your daughter was raised from the dead before your very own eyes, could you manage to remain quiet about it for very long—even if the Healer Himself had instructed you to say nothing? It may be possible, but it is pretty unlikely.

Throughout His ministry on earth, Jesus consistently exudes confidence and faith in His mission and Himself. He expresses, without hesitation, that He does what the Father wants Him to do (John 5:19; 8:28; 9:4). He stays true to His objectives, and remains personally unaffected by external factors; whether they be people's words or threats, incurable diseases, demonic forces, or even natural disasters. He is not reserved in His preaching or ministering to others. He is perceptive of other's faith and always ready to tend to the needs of all who come to Him. He does experience happiness, compassion, anger, disappointment—but these neither elevate nor destroy His purpose or singleness of mind. In essence, His confidence in Himself and God's plan helps drive Him forward. Essentially, his feelings do not affect how He sees Himself or his Ministry. He has sufficient self-esteem to do what He does, and His sense of purpose and worthiness is neither diminished nor improved by anyone or anything around Him.

Another fine example of Jesus' perspective of Himself is evident by His words and deeds in the temple at Jerusalem. (John 2:15) He was angry at how God's house had been turned into a marketplace for greedy opportunists. After making a small whip, He drove out all the animals being sold for sacrifices as well as the people selling them. To punctuate His point even more, He turned over all the sellers' tables, and accused them of changing the purposes of God's temple into a den for thieves (Matthew 21:13; Mark 11:17; Luke 19:46). This was an unequivocally aggressive action, and an equally bold statement to publicly make in the busiest and most travelled to location in the entire city. These are not the actions of a person who questions His identity or self-confidence. This is not what a self-doubting, insecure individual would say to a group of strangers who were not only accepted by the general population, but most certainly even respected and greatly admired by them.

Sidebar: While we can find no clear evidence that the temple's High Priest and his fellow priests partook of the market profits, it is almost a certainty that they sanctioned such activities. The temple was their domain, and the sellers of goods undoubtedly had to pay homage in the form of rent, percentage of sales, coerced "offerings", or some such tribute. Jesus was assailing the behavior of the temple priests probably even more than the moneychangers themselves. For it was the priests who were profiting most by deciding to turn the temple of God from a place of worship into an open marketplace. Among others, this particular event was likely one of the primary triggers for discussions to arrest and execute Jesus.

Jesus did not hesitate in His condemnation of those responsible for this violation of God's temple. He spoke with authority and certainty. He did not hold back. These are the actions and words of an individual who clearly and definitively knows who He is and also what His purpose is.

Perhaps one of the best arguments for the idea that Jesus' self-worth comes from God is found in John 5:30.

"I can of Myself do nothing. As I hear, I judge; and My judgment is righteous, because I do not seek My own will, but the will of the Father who sent me."

Jesus was God the Son—He knew it; He said it in so many words—yet He submitted Himself completely and entirely to the Father's will. He plainly stated that He was the personal representative for God the Father on this earth. He was secure in Himself, and His relationship with the Father. This was a powerful and significant statement, and should not be overlooked or regarded lightly.

> Sidebar: Please make an effort to study and meditate on all of the fifth chapter of John, particularly verses 19-47. This passage is where Jesus makes one of the most compelling presentations of who He is, and how He identifies with the Father. In essence, He accuses the Jewish rulers of not knowing Him, because they do not truly know God.

Jesus takes a multi-faceted approach to instructing the Jews about Himself. In combination, these events and arguments strike a decisive blow to the religious people who question His actions, authority, and teachings.

Jesus starts by healing the man at the pool of Bethesda, someone afflicted for thirty-eight years. (This action is an outward sign of His power.) Jesus then instructs him to take up his bed and walk—*on the Sabbath.* (A verbal indication of His authority as Lord of the Sabbath.) But Jewish leaders later see the man carrying his bed and they rebuke him, for Jewish doctrine strictly forbade any work on the Sabbath. The man replies that he was only obeying the words of the One who healed him (another subtle reference to the authority of Jesus).

In verse 16, they confront Jesus and accuse Him of violating religious laws. They actually were so angry, that they wanted to *kill* Him. In a somewhat veiled response, Jesus answers in verse 17 by essentially comparing Himself (and His works) to the Father. This makes the Jewish leaders even angrier. He then proceeds to emphasize His position with God by instructing them further.

In verse 19, He asserts *"I only do what the Father does."* If the Jewish rulers accept this statement as stated, then they must necessarily agree that Jesus is exercising the authority given Him by God. He is trying to instruct them that His actions, words, and behavior are all derived from His relationship with the Father. Plus, He is also effectively accusing them of not having the connection to the Father that they claim to have. For if they did, then they would recognize Jesus for who He is.

- In verses 22-23, Jesus says He has been given the authority to judge all things, and that those who do not honor Him, do not honor the Father.
- Verses 24-29 plainly refer to Jesus' authority to judge, and the power to give eternal life to those who honor the Son.
- In verse 30, He once again declares where His standing comes from when He says, *"I do the will of the Father who sent Me."*

Jesus then attempts to utilize John the Baptist, the Old Testament scriptures, and Moses to further augment His position. John was regarded as a great prophet by the Jews, and of course the scriptures and Moses were irreproachable in Jewish culture. He directly references them as witnesses to Him, saying that He is of whom they spoke. (John 5:33-47) In essence, He accuses the Jews of not knowing Him, because they do not truly know John, the scriptures, or Moses.

Finally, in a not-at-all subtle way, Jesus tells the Jewish leaders that they are not as learned and scholarly as they believe themselves to be. For if they were, they would know and recognize Him as God's Sent One. (We can assume that a man would have to be pretty comfortable with himself to openly say to the so-called *experts* that they really don't know the first thing about their chosen field of study; in this case, thousands of years' worth of Jewish religion and law.)

To summarize, it becomes abundantly clear that Jesus' sense of self, *and* of self-worth, were extraordinarily important in His actions, words, and ministry. His firm grasp of the knowledge that He was God's own Son, as well as His vital importance to fulfilling God's plan, were unmistakable and irrefutable. These certainties are, in part, what guided Him throughout His earthly ministry. The benefit we derive from this conviction is that we know, from Jesus' own words, that He desires the same confidence for us.

"I in them, and Thou in Me, that they may be made perfect in One; and that the world may know that Thou hast sent Me,

and hast loved them, as Thou hast loved Me." (John 17:23).

Jesus wants us to be like Him. He wants us to be confident in our knowledge of Him, confident in who He is, and equally confident of who we are in Him. He gave us an excellent example of this while still engaged in earthly ministry.

"And when He had called unto Him His twelve disciples, He gave them power against unclean spirits, to cast them out, and to heal all manner of sickness and all manner of disease." (Matthew 10:1)
"And He called unto Him the twelve, and began to send them forth two by two; and gave them power over unclean spirits." (Mark 6:7)

"After these things the Lord appointed other seventy also, and sent them two by two . . ." (Luke 10:1)
"And the seventy returned again with joy, saying, Lord, even the devils are subject unto us through thy name." (Luke 10:17)

The most notable thing about these events (which often remains unnoticed), is the fact that these people went out and did what they did *because He told them to.* They did not have to participate in any sort of specialized training or education. They did not have to prepare themselves in any way, or wait until they felt good enough, smart enough, or strong enough to act on His words. They did not practice casting out devils over and over again until they felt at ease with it, or until they felt like they "got it right". Jesus told

FRANK CASSO

them what to do—and they went out and did it. He esteemed them worthy to do the job, and then empowered them to go forth. His confidence was projected into them, and they received it, and then they acted upon it. This is a lesson we can all learn and be reminded of today. Jesus said it, and therefore it is so. Period . . . end of discussion. Just as Jesus knew who He was, He knew who they were. He did not depend on their personal self-assessments to see if they could get the job done. He did not interview or pre-qualify them as potential candidates who could handle the challenges of ministry. He imparted to them His power, His confidence, and His authority. That is where their assurance of success came from. So it was then . . . and so it still remains today.

Jesus has deemed us worthy, and it is entirely up to us to walk in that conviction—knowing that He has declared—that for all principalities, powers, and dominions; for all manner of sickness and disease; for every situation, *and in* every situation, that **we are His workmanship**, His vessels, His representatives on this earth.

Let us close this review of Jesus with possibly one of the most powerful statements He made while on earth—at least as it pertains to our topic of study.

"Verily, verily, I say unto you, he that believeth on Me, the works that I do shall he do also; and greater works than these shall he do; because I go unto my Father." (John 14:12)

As Christians, we marvel at the history of Jesus' acts: blind eyes opened, deaf ears made to hear, the dead raised back to life, the demoniac delivered, the lame made whole, Jesus walking on water, the stilling of the storm, and on and on. This is quite an impressive and inspirational portfolio of works. And yet in light of what He tells us in John 14:12, it causes us to pause and examine ourselves. We are His—new creatures in Christ (II Corinthians 5:17), Believers in His death and resurrection as well as the Redeemer of mankind, all for the glory of God. *We* believe on Him. But are we doing the works that He spoke of? I confess that I haven't done most of what Jesus did. I believe it, I agree with it, but I'm not living it.

Sidebar: Remember Romans 8:1? There is no reason to feel guilt, shame, condemnation, or any other negative emotion about your mistakes, failures, or missed opportunities. Seek forgiveness and move past them—God will do the same.

So let's just all walk on water, out onto the middle of the lake to prove that we are able to do what Jesus said, shall we? Now that would be just plain silly. Jesus never did anything to show off or grandstand; and we should follow that example. Everything He did was intended to minister to others, or to expedite and convey God's message of love and redemption. In that context, we are basically tasked by the Lord Himself to imitate Him.

It is incredibly important to us, and our future actions as Christians to truly understand that *we* are

the disciples . . . *we* are among the seventy being sent
. . . *we* are the Believer(s) of whom Jesus speaks about
in John 14:12. I say this not to challenge you to go out
and begin raising the dead to life. (Although if that is
what God is calling you to do, then by all means, do
it!) The larger point here is that Jesus is sending us
forth in *His* faith. We are to mimic Him, just as He
says in John 5:19 that He mimicked the Father. Jesus
knows that we will be confronted with self-doubt,
unbelief, and the adversities of poor self-esteem. That
is why He said to *believe on Him.* That is where, and
from whom, the strength of our being comes.
Understand that our own feelings about ourselves will
never affect or influence <u>His</u> opinion about us.

Sidebar: Feelings can be wonderful and marvelous, but
they are often misleading or fickle. Jesus had feelings
too. He wept; He felt compassion; He was angry at the
moneychangers. But His feelings never determined
the "right-ness" of His actions or words. Here's an
example to emphasize the point. We know from
scripture that Jesus will physically return to set up His
kingdom on earth for a thousand years. That
knowledge inevitability implies and assures us that the
yellow sun up in the sky will come up tomorrow . . . and
the next day . . . and the next. No amount of human
interference, man-made space junk, massive sun
flares, or celestial bodies hurtling through space can
prevent the rising of the sun. It is a certainty. It is an
absolute. And anyone who "feels" like that could
somehow be prevented by man, or change on its own,
or just outright believe that it will not happen at all, is

---

only wasting their time, effort, or resources worrying about the immovable and unchangeable. The sun rising each day has been established <u>by God</u>, and it shall not cease . . . *ever* . . . until He tells it to.

Since the Lord is not swayed or deterred by our shortcomings, He has a greater sense of who we are than we do about ourselves. He projects Himself to us, and through us; just as He did with His disciples and the seventy. It is therefore logical that we should rely on Him as our source for our self-esteem.

To use a silly but effective illustration with which we are all familiar as children, (and some of us as parents) Jesus is practically telling us "Because I say so." We are good enough and capable enough to fulfill His desires for us for the simplest and best reason possible: The Lord of all creation, the Redeemer of all mankind, the Savior of the world has said to you and me, "—*Insert your own name here*—, you *are* worthy because I say you are. I made you to be more than you thought you could be. And I believe in you because I am sending you out with My faith, and in My power, and that is far greater than you just having faith in your own human abilities." ("*Without Me, you can do nothing.*" (John 15:5)

Are there more examples of Jesus referencing His words and deeds to the Father's? Absolutely.

"*And there are many other things which Jesus did, the which, if they should be written every one, I suppose that not even the world itself could contain the books that should be written. Amen.*" (John 21:25)

We have merely examined a fraction of the recorded ones to support our position that Jesus was unquestionably sure of who He is, and what He had to do while in His earthly ministry. All during that time, and even today, He instructs us to believe as He does, so that we can be freed from the paralyzing burdens and heavy weights of self-pity, shame, and low self-esteem. He wants us to rise above these so that we can be fruitful and productive ambassadors for His kingdom; so that we can reach others, and so that our joy may be full.

The Self-Esteem of Moses

Many of us who consider Moses will inevitably recall the famous movie depiction by an actor who set a high standard for this story and its genre. (We cannot name the movie or actor without proper permission, but the movie was released in 1956 and the actor's initials are "C.H.") In some respects, this portrayal is representative of the biblical Moses. From a storytelling perspective, it is reasonably accurate, although it is limited in that you cannot tell the whole story of a remarkable man who lived one hundred and twenty years in just a three hour movie. Some artistic license (relative to actual scripture) was taken with events in the story, but we recommend you watch it anyway for inspirational and entertainment purposes.

As we know, the baby Moses was carefully set adrift in a basket in the river (presumably the Nile). His mother did this to protect him from the slaughter Pharaoh had ordered to destroy all the recently born male children because Israel, even though harshly oppressed, was growing stronger as a people. (Exodus 1:9, 22) Pharaoh's daughter found him and raised him as her own son. (Exodus 2:5) For the next number of years, Moses lived his life as a prince of Egypt. He enjoyed the finest foods, had the most exotic of experiences, and wore luxurious clothes woven from expensive cloths and adorned with precious metals and rare jewels. As a member of the royal house, his education was second to none. There were few in all of Egypt who were his equal, and even fewer that he answered to. The most powerful nation and people of the world esteemed and regarded Moses highly, and he reaped all the benefits of that position of earthly honor.

However, as God's plan would have it, in a short period of time, Moses went from prince to criminal to fugitive. (Exodus 2:11-15) Moses walked among his people to contemplate the harshness of their existence, and happened upon an Egyptian beating a Hebrew. He was angry at what he saw, and in a fit of rage, killed the Egyptian. The very next day, he was accused and verbally scorned by another Hebrew about the killing. Moses realized that the murder he committed was not a secret, and he fled for his life once Pharaoh learned of it, and sought to kill him.

It is not at all unreasonable to assume that Moses had now lost every bit of self-esteem he had. His complete and utter crash from such a lofty and revered position of honor must have been devastating. He left his home and everything he knew as he escaped to the land of Midian. However, as God's plan unfolded, he met and then helped several sisters drawing water for their flocks. (Exodus 2:15-21) Their father was grateful and after a time, offered one of his daughters in marriage to Moses. For the next number of years, this former Prince of Egypt lived the very unglamorous life of a shepherd—a far cry from his old one back in the house of Pharaoh. For Moses, this must have surely been a period for self-reflection and soul-searching. Surely, it was during this time that his self-esteem shifted away from being propped up by privilege, riches, and a deference to royalty, to being embedded in hard work, a simple lifestyle, and personal humility. Only after this internal transformation would God use Moses to implement the next phase of His plan for Israel.

In Exodus Chapter 3 is where we see God personally engage and communicate with Moses for the first time. The story of the burning bush that was not consumed by fire is among the most famous of Old Testament stories. Here, God explains:

1) who He is,
2) what Moses should do,
3) how he will carry out God's plan, and
4) what the final outcome will be.

Notice that Moses actually responded to God. No doubt he did so with the utmost respect and reverence.

<u>Sidebar</u>: In Exodus 3:11 & 13, Moses actually had the boldness to question God. However, he didn't ask disrespectfully, but rather in meekness so he could understand his assigned mission better. The point for us here is that God does not necessarily want us to be clueless about His plans for our lives. If we ask, He will give us whatever information or clarification we may need to take the next step. But this does not mean He is required to fully explain every aspect of what He wants us to do. It is likely that if we knew the entirety of God's plan for our lives, because of our imperfections, we would probably find some way of sabotaging it ourselves. Often God will dispense specific information and instructions to us on an as-needed basis. In this way, it is less likely we will attempt to alter His plans by infusing our own ideas or opinions into the mix. This also serves to keep the enemy off-balance as he remains largely unaware of the logistics and mechanics of God's plan unfolding in our lives.

Most notable to us is Exodus 3:11, *"And Moses said unto God, Who am I, that I should go unto Pharaoh, and that I should bring forth the children of Israel out of Egypt?"* Although it had been many years since living in Pharaoh's house, Moses was not unaware of the power and authority of the ruler of the greatest nation on earth. We could examine Moses' thinking behind this question in several different ways.

It could be that Moses now thought so little of himself that he doubted his own ability to even stand before Pharaoh, much less demand the release of Israel. Or perhaps he feared being taken captive and executed for his crime from so many years before. Either of these could certainly shake the self-confidence of any man. Lastly, it is unlikely that Moses doubted who God was and that He was speaking to him, but it is still somewhat unusual that Moses actually needed some explanation and convincing that God was in control and had everything planned out. If any (or all) of these were true, it would be quite difficult to muster up the courage and self-confidence necessary to move forward. This makes it obvious to us that God had to be Moses' active supporter, coach, and cheerleader. Exodus 4 starts with the self-doubt and reservation Moses had about the whole thing. God had to conduct a show of the miraculous in order to bolster Moses' confidence (Exodus 4:2-7). Even then, Moses resisted and doubted God's decision to choose him. In Exodus 4:10-17, God confirmed that He had chosen Moses; then He became angry with him for still trying to figure a way out of this task.

This is a prime example of how we often decide that God must be wrong when He chooses us to do something for Him. We squirm, we resist, and then we try our hardest to figure a means of escape. (I suppose it is only God's infinite grace and love that keeps Him from becoming so very impatient and angry with us.) Like Moses, we doubt ourselves. We doubt our calling. We question God's decision to choose us. We expect or demand evidence now that He will support us moving forward. This level of doubt in who God is, and why He has selected us can be poisonous to fulfilling our missions for God. That is why it is absolutely critical and truly imperative that we draw our sense of worth and self-esteem from Him. He has decided that we are His choice for whatever mission or ministry or service. That ought to be enough for us, and should be the banner under which we take action. God has deemed us worthy, and we should not dishonor how He esteems us by disrespecting His plan, or His choices (you and me) for carrying out His will.

In the chapters that follow (Exodus 5-12), Moses carries out that which God has called him to do. It is not without difficulty or challenge, but God has ordained the end result, and His plans will not be undone by mere men. Once Moses got into agreement, and then subsequently into the flow of God's power, he was able to fulfill his role. The point for us to take away from this is that Moses had to shed his own self-assessments and his own personal sense of value first. He had to no longer regard himself, but rather solely rely on how God saw him. Then he was able to incorporate into his own thinking how God valued him. That is what made the difference between Moses the shepherd, and Moses the sent deliverer of God's people.

Sidebar: Let us suggest that you study the whole of Moses' life in Exodus, Numbers, and Deuteronomy. There are multiple reasons for doing so. First, there is the study of how this man came to be the liberator that God sent to free Israel. Of course, the Ten Commandments and all the subsequent laws ordained by God are the foundation of the Old Testament and Covenant. The construction of the Ark of the Covenant and what that spiritually represents is of paramount interest and importance to Believers even to this day. And there is more to learn about: the miracles of manna, water from the rock, the first look at the Promised Land, the forty years of sojourning in the wilderness, prophecies and foreshadowing of the Messiah, and much, much more.

Throughout Moses' remaining years on earth, there were highs and lows, progress and setbacks, triumphs and frustrations. Yet overall, he continued to grow and flourish in his position as the leader of Israel. These instances illustrate how a person can be flawed and very "*human*", and yet still serve God quite ably. Moses had many opportunities to fail and even quit, but he did not. Had he chosen to rely on his own self-esteem, none of these miraculous and wonderful things would have ever occurred. It is clear that Moses was the man that he was because of the value that God placed *on* him, and *in* him, and throughout his life Moses put that Godly self-esteem into action again and again.

The Self-Esteem of the Roman Centurion

In the book of Luke (Chapter 7:2-10) we learn of a Roman Centurion who besought Jesus to heal a much loved servant. To give this story its proper perspective, let us first remember that Judaea was a conquered land under foreign control. The Roman Empire was unlike any other up until that time in history. The kingdom of Caesar fully encompassed the entire Mediterranean Sea, including most of western and southern Europe, the entire coast of North Africa, southeastern Europe, into the Middle East, and even reaching into western Asia. No country or people could withstand the advancing armies of Rome. The might and authority of Caesar could not at all be challenged by lesser kingdoms.

Now this Roman Centurion was most probably a battle-tested and hardened soldier. It is certain that he had fought well and shown strong leadership to achieve his rank. A Centurion (military leader of a century of men (meaning one hundred)) usually did not ascend to this position of authority except by having earned it. And it would also be true that he was well aware and well-practiced in fitting into the chain of command of such a mighty and successful army.

It would be no surprise that a man of such accomplishment would have a sense of certitude about his own position in life and society. You could not achieve such a prominent and desirable station by doubting yourself and your own worth. This Roman Centurion had likely endured much adversity and war during his lifetime, and was sure of who he was and what he could and could not do. Further, while this is pure speculation on our part, it is possible that he was located in Judaea as a reward for many years of faithful service to the Emperor. (The Jewish lands had been conquered for many decades by Christ's time. There were still occasional uprisings and rebellions, but a somewhat stable, albeit tenuous peace had been established.) Moreover, this Centurion had obviously been in the area long enough to earn the respect and admiration of the local Jewish elders. They spoke to Jesus of this man saying, *"For he loveth our nation, and he hath built us a synagogue."* (Luke 7:5)

Now that we have some historical and societal perspective, let us examine the story more closely. When the Centurion had heard of Jesus, he sent word to Him by way of Jewish elders, imploring Him to come and heal a dear servant who was close to death. These elders deemed this Roman worthy of Christ's attention because of his honorable dealings towards the Jews.

Sidebar: Some believe that this Centurion was the same one who said in Matthew 27:54 *"Truly this was the Son of God"* when Jesus died on the Cross. We cannot verify the truthfulness of this notion. But it seems reasonable, even likely that this was the case. Whether it was the same man, or not, it is an interesting thought to think that perhaps the Roman Centurion(s) may have actually become Believer(s) at a time when Christianity was first considered as a faith of government subversives and religious outlaws.

As Jesus approached the Centurion's home, he was met by friends who stopped Him from entering the man's house. *"Lord, trouble not thyself: for I am not worthy that thou shouldest enter under my roof. . ."* was the message sent to Jesus. Here was a mighty man of war, a leader of men, a powerful member of the occupying army of Rome, and he recognizes and defers to Jesus as a spiritual leader and miracle worker. He even honors Jesus by calling him "Lord", which is an acknowledgement of his respect and admiration. Then he states that he is not even worthy enough to have the Lord enter his house. It is notable that he and his countrymen were the conquerors, and yet he was ashamed to have Jesus even come into his home!

Then the Centurion reiterates his respect to Jesus by going further. *"Wherefore neither thought I myself worthy to come unto thee . . ."* How is it that this accomplished and respected soldier and leader of the powerful Roman army considers that his standing does not at all compare to the greatness he perceives in Jesus? It is because he recognizes power. He recognizes authority. He sees and hears of the evidence confirming the greatness of Christ. And that is what led him to say, *". . . but say in a word, and my servant shall be healed. For I also am a man set under authority, having under me soldiers, and I say unto one, Go, and he goeth; and to another, Come, and he cometh; and to my servant, Do this, and he doeth it."*

Now understand that this man's personal self-esteem was not lacking. He was a man of stature. He was a man of considerable reputation. And yet he did not regard his own esteem when it came time to seek something from Jesus. He knew that, comparatively speaking, he was nothing when matched up against the authority and power of this Man of God. He may not yet have fully realized that Jesus was God's own Son, but he surely saw that this was no ordinary man.

"When Jesus heard these things, He marvelled . . . and turned . . . and said unto the people that followed . . . 'I say unto you, I have not found so great faith, no, not in Israel'." Though the Centurion may not have fully understood, his esteem and respect for Jesus and His authority amazed the Lord. Jesus regarded and valued this man's esteem towards Him, and then reciprocated. *"And they that were sent, returning to the house, found the servant whole that had been sick."*

This Centurion, not lacking in or doubting his own earthly position, set aside his own self-esteem to seek the help of One who was greater. It is reasonable to think that God had probably not infused this man beforehand with any measure of spiritual value. Rather, because of his background and training, the Centurion quite naturally esteemed what he perceived to be a greater and divine power. His own humility and faith, along with his recognition of higher authority was what facilitated Jesus fulfilling his request.

We would do ourselves a great service to see our own situations and circumstances as this Centurion did. We can acknowledge the grace of God, the authority of Jesus, and the power of the Holy Spirit to move and therefore act in our best interest. We can ask humbly as this Roman did, but even better, we can seek God's help because we have been adopted into God's own family. (*"For ye have not received the spirit of bondage again to fear; but ye have received the Spirit of adoption, whereby we cry, Abba, Father."* (Romans 8:15)). It is that relationship that gives us a far superior (and more desirable) position for seeking His help and direction. For, unlike the Roman Centurion, we not only see the great authority of God, but more significantly, we know that we are His children. We have a right to access Him in time of need—not because of who we are, but because He sees us as His own. That is what He desires for us—that is, for us to value ourselves as He values us.

The Self-Esteem of the Canaanite Woman

As Christians, we often think too much with our heads, and don't listen with our hearts. We may give mental or verbal assent to what we've learned or been taught to believe, but that knowledge may not have the rock-solid and fixed standing it deserves in our lives. (That normally comes with study, prayer, meditation, maturity, and more prayer. The Holy Spirit will teach us as we go along, but it is the regular exercising of our spiritual selves that continuously builds our faith and knowledge, making us ever stronger in the Lord.)

Does this mushiness of spirit affect our self-esteem? Of course it does. When we feel down or low, we tend to let those feelings influence how we see ourselves. That, in turn, affects what we say, how we do things, and how we minister to others. Can we ever reach a place of assurance where this no longer adversely affects our self-image, thoughts, or actions? Theoretically speaking, yes. Realistically speaking, yes. Practically speaking, yes. But it does not necessarily happen quickly, or without some resistance or challenge. Ultimately, it is the persistence of our faith walk that eventually yields the rewards of walking in faith. To illustrate some of these truths, let us examine the story of the Canaanite woman in Matthew 15:22-28.

Verse 22 begins *". . . a woman of Canaan came out . . . and cried unto Him, saying, "Have mercy on me, O Lord, thou son of David; my daughter is grievously vexed with a devil."* Here was a woman who probably had great difficulty getting through the crowd, so she called out loudly to Him to get His attention. (Verses 31 & 38 talk of the multitude, and numbers the men at four thousand, plus women and children. This was quite a large group of people to navigate through.) She plainly, clearly, and boldly

1. asked for mercy,
2. acknowledged Him as Lord,
3. recognized Him as a descendant of the great King David,
4. and requested her daughter's deliverance.

This Canaanite woman was from an inferior race (thought to be so by the Jewish leaders of the day), who had heard that Jesus was passing through. She did not let what others think deter her from seeking His help. Neither did she give in to any sense of doubt or self-pity. She was on a mission to get healing for her daughter, and wasn't going to be stopped by feelings, emotions, or even racial prejudice.

"But He answered her not a word." Jesus had multiple and very good reasons for not responding.

Firstly, the woman sought mercy from Jesus. In order to give mercy, one has to have the power to do so. She had certainly heard of Jesus and His ministry. Otherwise, why seek Him out in the first place? Her request for His mercy actually proclaimed to everyone nearby that He was truly capable of granting it.

Secondly, she called him *Lord*. She did not call Him master or teacher. She did not call Him prophet or rabbi. She called Him **_Lord_**. Once again, this was for the benefit of all who were following. Further, she linked "mercy" with "Lord" and attributed both of these to Jesus. Until that time, this was a characteristic and a name that was reserved for God alone. This would turn out to be another public declaration of who Jesus was.

Thirdly, she called Him the Son of David. In earthly terms, there was already tremendous meaning and deference to being a descendant of King David. But more significantly, being called the "Son of David" was a reference with messianic overtones. The

Canaanite woman effectively and openly declared
Jesus as the Messiah in no uncertain terms.

Lastly, she beseeched Him on behalf of her
daughter, who was *"grievously vexed with a devil"*. The fall
of Lucifer and his followers was commonly known in
Old Testament times. Here, she acknowledged Jesus
as being superior in power and strength compared to
the power of the enemy. Hence, another roundabout
declaration of His position of authority.

*"And His disciples came and besought Him, saying, 'Send
her away; for she crieth after us'."* The implication here is
that the Canaanite woman was making a nuisance of
herself. Her constant cries and pleas were at least
distracting, if not completely irritating. The disciples
recognized that Jesus was apparently not going to do
anything to help her, so they figured that He would
silence and rebuke her, then send her away. Strangely,
Jesus only answered, *"I am not sent but unto the lost sheep
of the house of Israel."*

Sidebar: At first glance, it appears that Jesus was
disinterested in helping this woman. His statement
even seems to border on and affirm the Jewish racism
of the day. But this is the natural and human way of
analyzing His remark. Everything that Jesus said had
deeper significance and meaning. First, He said He was
sent only to the house of Israel. But this statement
does not preclude God from ever sending others to
minister to the rest of the world. (The writings of Paul,
Peter, and John later address the issue of God's grace
being available for all of mankind. It is later explained

quite plainly that Jesus' sacrifice was intended for everyone.) Jesus also indirectly confirmed His mission as implied by the Canaanite woman's public statements. He references Isaiah 53, most specifically verse 6 by referring to the *"lost sheep"*. Isaiah 53 is noted as one of the most profound and significant scriptures foretelling the coming of the Messiah. This was another clever way of stating who He was.

What an odd response to a specific request! No doubt the disciples looked at one another with puzzled faces, trying to decipher what Jesus meant by His answer. We can only understand it ourselves if we consider the context of the time and event.

Jesus was trying to teach His disciples. He wasn't just performing miracles. He was always instructing them, and indirectly us, as to who He was and why He was there. In part, the reason He allowed her to go on with her repetitious words was to allow her to proclaim who He was. She was declaring Jesus to the throng of people following. She was confirming Jesus as Messiah to His very own disciples. And most importantly of all, she was pronouncing Him as the Sent One of God to the Pharisees, Sadducees, and Jewish rulers who were following Him; some primarily for the purpose of exposing Jesus as a false prophet. In short, the Canaanite woman was **preaching** to the masses, the disciples, and the Jewish clergy about Jesus, His authority, and His mission on earth!

To top it all off, then she came and ". . . *worshipped Him, saying, 'Lord, help me'.*" She punctuated her "sermon" by engaging in what we all could do more of—worshipping the Lord.

"But He answered and said, 'It is not meet to take the children's bread, and to cast it to dogs'." This was a beautiful and clever setup by Jesus. Initially, it seems to indicate that He agreed with Jewish laws and customs which clearly scorned the notion of anyone other than the Jews being God's people. It was a religious racism that had prevailed for over a thousand years. He was letting the Jewish clergy know that He was familiar with their doctrines and beliefs, and at first, it seemed that He agreed with them.

"And she said, 'Truth, Lord: yet the dogs eat of the crumbs which fall from their masters' table'." Her point was that even dogs have the right to benefit somewhat from what is available from their masters. Again, the woman was unintentionally instructing those present that God's mercies and benefits can be extended to everyone who humbly seek Him.

Sidebar: There is evidence in the Old Testament that confirms that it was possible for a non-Israeli or non-Jew to convert if they embraced the Jewish laws and customs. Unfortunately, we do not have the time to expound upon this here. But let us say that this possibility is actually a type of foreshadowing of the New Testament. Since any person could convert to Judaism under the Old Covenant, and any person can now become a Christian under the New Covenant.

"Then Jesus answered and said unto her, 'O woman, great is thy faith: be it unto thee even as thou wilt'. And her daughter

was made whole from that very hour."

Jesus acknowledged and respected her exchange. He honored her by recognizing her faith and granting her petition. And He did so knowing that everyone present would contemplate her words, and realize that He was indeed the Sent One of God. Additionally, He indicated that it was faith that was required to grasp who and what He was.

In summary, this Canaanite woman had no social, political, or financial standing to approach the Lord— much less ask for a free gift of mercy and healing. She referred to herself as a dog in the masters' house. But she knew that even that lowly position had certain value and benefits. She was not deterred by a lack of self-esteem. For she knew that her own self-value had little to do with Jesus' ability to help her. She recognized Him for who He was, and counted on His mercy and grace to supply an answer for her need. In the process, the woman was used mightily by God to instruct the people, the disciples, and even the Jewish religious leaders present. It was the certainty of God's value of her that helped her pursue and receive the blessings she desired.

These champions of the Bible represent but a fraction of the stories of ordinary people (Jesus excluded) who had to put their own sense of worth aside. We include in this gallery of heroes Paul and Elijah, both of whom are mentioned elsewhere in this book. There are many other examples of course, but this substantially supports the premise that we must intentionally put our Godly self-esteem into action so that we may derive the benefits of that effort.

However, we must regularly practice drawing our self-esteem from Him. It is incumbent on us to consistently remind ourselves through scripture, prayer, and self-discipline in our words and deeds. That will help us be ready to prepare, counter, and ultimately overcome, the mental and spiritual assaults of the world and the enemy.

6

YOUR SELF-ESTEEM
AND YOUR FREE WILL

God created us in His own image (Genesis 1:27). Adam was created to fellowship *with* God, not specifically to serve Him. God gave him the ability to make that choice. He endowed him with the power to decide for himself what he should and should not do. Unlike the angels who were created for the distinct purpose of serving God, Adam had the unique capacity to determine whether or not to engage in a relationship with his Father. (see *"Adam, which was the son of God"* (Luke 3:38)) As we all now know, Adam gave up that direct and intimate fellowship when he sinned against God because of his own willful disobedience.

Sidebar #1 – The Bible tells us plainly that the woman was deceived, but Adam was not (I Timothy 2:14). For all those who proclaim that Eve was at fault for man's downfall, it is patently unfair (and unscriptural) to solely blame her. Quite simply, she was lied to, and subsequently tricked, into eating the forbidden fruit of the Tree of Knowledge of Good and Evil. Yes, she could have said no, but the fact that she did not in no way absolves Adam from his own <u>intentional</u> act of disobedience. **He** was the keeper of the Garden, and he was the one who had received clear instruction on this matter directly from God—<u>before</u> the woman had even been created (Genesis 2:16-17)

<u>Sidebar #2</u> – Sometimes, we imagine that Adam—who had EVERYTHING he could possibly want or need—was such a fool for violating the one and only restriction that God had placed on him. I'll not argue the point, other than to say that it is quite easy for us to denounce Adam for his apparent folly. However, the reality is that most of us, perhaps even all of us, likely would have done the same thing. It is in our nature to choose because God created us with that ability. But it is also all too easy for us to be enticed away from things that are righteous and Godly. The opportunity to choose is a great gift from God, but it comes with an even greater responsibility to choose correctly and in a holy manner.

This is often where Christians "mess up". For it is a veritable certainty that every Christian will, at some point, falter or fail in some way. A private, secret sin is no less objectionable to God than an outwardly brazen or public one. A one-time, rare, or occasional sin is as distasteful and unsavory to Him as those that are habitual or committed on a larger scale. Different sins will have different effects and variable consequences on us, our loved ones, our careers, etc., whether they be committed in secret, or are open and visible for scrutiny. Nevertheless, from God's perspective, all sin is abominable and must be dealt with appropriately.

That is why we have Jesus – to *"take away the sin of the world."* (John 1:29)

So then, let's review:

- God created Adam with free will and the ability to choose.
- It was Adam's choice to disobey God, thus condemning all of mankind.
- Everyone is now free to accept God's forgiveness through Jesus Christ.
- After our salvation, we are still capable of choosing *to sin* . . . or *not* to sin.
- Every Christian will sin at least once during their Christian walk.

It seems like free will and the ability to choose is truly a double-edged sword, one that cuts deeply and both ways. On the one hand, we get to remediate an ugly choice that was made by Adam (for us) without our consent or participation. That decision restores us to a personal relationship and right-standing with God, which is what He originally intended.

On the other hand, we will inevitably forget or ignore, perhaps even intentionally set aside, that association and position of righteousness for fleeting moments of personal indulgence and selfish satisfaction.

Paul referenced these struggles in his own life. *"O wretched man that I am! who shall deliver me from the body of this death?"* (Romans 7:14-24) He was clearly dealing with some of the same internal conflicts and personal turmoil that every Christian contends with. And yet, he was, and still is, universally recognized as an eminent scholar of the Christ and the New Covenant. Even Peter, an Apostle who personally walked and talked with Jesus wrote about Paul's writings: *". . . our beloved brother Paul also according to the wisdom given unto him . . . in all his epistles . . . are some things hard to be understood . . ."* (II Peter 3:15-16)

How is it that Paul can possibly be both a failure **and** a primary example of a Christian leader? Remember, Paul (Saul) was the man who held the coats of those who stoned Stephen to martyrdom, as he looked on approvingly. (Acts 7:58-59) (Would not an action like this clearly define the man forever?)

Additionally, why would God bless and honor the works and writings of a man who called himself *"chief among sinners"*? (I Timothy 1:15) (Apparently, even after his conversion, Paul had some guilt and regret over his sins and failings.)

However in another passage, what is it that prompts this same flawed man to have the confidence to suggest of himself, *"He that glorieth, let him glory in the*

Lord?" (I Corinthians 1:31) (Bragging is rarely looked upon favorably, and yet Paul was not timid in asserting his position and his personal relationship with the Lord. (I Corinthians 1:23-31))

Finally, by what authority does Paul have the audacity to declare the following: *"So say I now again, if any man preach any other gospel unto you than that ye have received (from me, Paul), let him be accursed."* (Galatians 1:9) (At first glance, this statement appears to be the height of narcissism and arrogance. It seems to even border on being judgmental to the point of severely excluding insights and revelation from others, effectively condemning them for their theological differences.)

Sidebar: Initially, Paul's confidence and conviction in his own preaching of the Christ and subsequent Christian doctrine sounds nothing short of arrogant and egotistical. Of that there is no doubt. However, we encourage you to study Paul's writings extensively. He has clearly and definitively laid out certain truths and absolutes that are supported and borne out in both Old Testament and New Testament scripture. Yet still, the question may be posed by some skeptics, "How can Paul be so sure of himself?" The answer is simple. The Lord wanted this information about Himself and His message to reach all generations. It had to be taught and distributed by someone. Paul was God's best, and first, choice to be the messenger of certain parts of Christian doctrine. *"Go thy way: for he is a chosen vessel unto me, to bear my name before the Gentiles, and kings, and the children of Israel."* (Acts 9:15)

> Paul was hand-picked by the Lord to fulfill this mission. Therefore, who is anyone to question Jesus' selection of Paul as His messenger; or the content of his teachings and writings?

Paul acknowledges that he is a sinner and unworthy of God's favor. But on the other hand, he is unambiguously stating that he does esteem himself highly – to the extent that he is not at all unclear about his position and stature as not only a Christian, but as a forerunner and purveyor of the faith. This contrasting dichotomy may be perplexing to those who have not experienced, (and therefore cannot truly comprehend) God's limitless forgiveness and grace. It is Christ Himself who has provided a blameless identity to Paul. Paul knows this, and he is absolutely confident and comfortable with the free gifts of righteousness and grace given to him by the Lord Jesus.

Paul portrays a principal example of a person who desires to serve God wholly, and without hesitation, reservation, or blemish. He is at peace with his standing with God, and rests in that surety of sonship. Conversely, he also exemplifies a person who has setbacks, shortcomings, and flaws. How can the two diverse and opposing personas co-exist in one man?

"So then with the mind I myself serve the law of God; but with the flesh the law of sin." (Romans 7:25)

The incredible truth here (and by the way, there are many others) is that Paul is both saint *and* sinner. He is able to fiercely proclaim and defend the faith, regardless of any personal inadequacies, because he plainly sees his righteous relationship with God as one that is established and completely anchored in who Jesus is, and what He has done. And although Paul has, at times, exercised his freedom to engage in actions that sometimes result in selfish or sinful events, he never wavers from the certainty of God's grace and power to sustain their relationship. He understands the quality of his righteousness is not predicated on his own behavior. Rather, it is preserved by Christ alone. It cannot be fouled or diminished by what Paul does, or does not do.

So then, we must ask the following questions: If Paul himself struggled with his own actions and/or behaviors, and yet was still confident of his salvation and right-standing with God, how can we possibly fare any worse? Should we dismiss the idea to willfully keep ourselves from sin, since we will most probably do no better than Paul the Apostle? As he implies, if our righteousness is actually dependent upon Christ and not on ourselves, can we not therefore conduct our lives in any way we desire or please?

No. It is all too easy to be drawn into sin if we know that Jesus has forgiven, and will continue, to forgive us. We may begin to flirt with sinful behaviors, all the while knowing that Jesus is there to restore us; that the Father is ready to take us back to place a ring on our finger and a fine robe on our backs. But this knowledge does not preclude us from taking an active role in conducting ourselves in a righteous manner.

We are clearly warned against this very enticing trap. Peter reminds us that God says to *"Be ye holy; for I am holy."* (I Peter 1:16) Paul said *"But I keep under my body, and bring it into subjection . . ."* (I Corinthians 9:27) intending that we should follow his example of self-discipline and self-control. He also instructed us to *"present your bodies a living sacrifice, holy, acceptable unto God, which is your reasonable service,"* (Romans 12:1) because we were *"bought with a price".* (I Corinthians 6:20) These passages encourage Believers to actively participate in a personal effort to remain holy and blameless before the Lord. It is within the scope and expectations of our personal Christianity to devote ourselves to this endeavor. To dismiss this obligation, particularly without any thought or consideration, is selfish and prideful. We may not always personally succeed, but like Paul, we must always be mindful to work towards that objective.

Additionally, Paul tells us *"Be ye followers of me, even as I also am of Christ."* (I Corinthians 11:1) So then, while he readily admits to his own shortcomings and failures, he confidently and plainly believes that these faults do not define who he is, nor what his relationship with the Lord is. It's almost as if Paul has permanently thrown off the shackles of sin, guilt, and shame because he realizes Jesus has freed him. Paul seems to only be affected by these in that they are temporary hindrances to furthering his relationship with God, as well as promoting Jesus Christ. Certainly evident is the knowledge and realization that Paul derives his self-worth from Jesus, *and only Jesus.* Paul's own actions and words, whether they be for the Kingdom, or in service to sin, do not define his inherent value to God. They do not affect his adoption into God's family. Though he may break the heart of his Father, God is ready to receive him back and restore him to his position of grace and honor. Like the Prodigal, Paul never ceases to be a son, regardless of what he may have done that is not pleasing to his Father. *This is the greatest distinction between Paul and the Prodigal.* The Prodigal believed that he ceased to be a son because of his selfish actions and poor decisions. Paul implies that he remains a son, *in spite* of his selfish actions and poor decisions. This is the liberation of mind that Paul wants us to understand. *"So with the mind I myself serve the law of God; but with my flesh the law of sin."* (Romans 7:25) Paul can still be effective as a witness for Christ, regardless of his own personal flaws and failures.

So if we are to "follow after Paul", then we must also embrace the understanding that our own relationship with God is established by Him. It is not contingent on what we do or don't do; what we say or don't say. It is supported and defined by, and relies solely upon, the Lord.

Now therefore, we truly have the freedom to choose how we live. We can either honor Jesus' sacrifice and ongoing ministry, or we can decide to continue in our own selfish (and often destructive) ways. But then, we have <u>always</u> had that power to choose. We were created with it. We exercise it when we closely follow God's ways; or when we stray from

His plan and desires for us. Yet we now can fully realize that our obedience to God is a gift that we can return to Him, as well as give to ourselves. How could we possibly not want what our Creator and Heavenly Father desires for us? If we would just set aside our pride and selfish lusts, there would be no other choice we would ever want to make.

"I call heaven and earth to record this day against you, that I have set before you life and death, blessing and cursing: therefore choose life." (Deuteronomy 30:19)

Once we realize that our life and our very "sonship" is rooted and established in Him, and by Him, we are freer to make the decisions and choices that honor God, rather than those that may shame our testimony. Equally important, is the firm knowledge and certainty that how we view ourselves is far less important than how we are viewed by God. Our value with the Father is not in jeopardy, so we can take comfort and assurance in knowing that we are worth much more than we could have ever believed or thought possible.

Brothers and sisters of the faith, it is well past time to see ourselves as He sees us. And as we do, our individual free will becomes more able and willing to align with the heart and mind of God.

Let us each endeavor to give to Him what He so desires most: that we follow, love, and adore Him *because we <u>choose</u> to.*

7

YOUR SELF-ESTEEM
AND YOUR FEELINGS

There is a lightning fast and direct connection between how we feel, and what we think about ourselves. One moment, we may feel like we can take on and prevail against whatever the world throws our way. Our emotions may ride high with a powerful sense of worth, achievement, or triumph. Yet within moments, we can feel alone, unloved, unwanted, a total failure, or worse—often as a result of bad news or some other unexpected personal setback. Every one of us has experienced emotional highs and lows; mood swings that quickly turn negative or positive because of a mean word, a generous deed, a sneer of disgust, or an overt expression of delight.

Our feelings are important. They help us to gauge ourselves, those around us, and the situations we encounter in daily life. Without them, we could not understand nor properly appreciate the warm embrace of a loving mother or child, the risks of engaging in an extreme sport like skydiving, or the pleasant satisfaction of having completed a difficult or challenging task well. It is obvious that God wanted us to experience the absolute pleasure and utility of emotions, since it is He who created them in us. Just like arms and legs, just like hearing and sight, God's aim was to give us the ability to fully enjoy our surroundings, our loved ones, and our achievements. Unfortunately, like the mind and body, our emotions can be tampered with or affected in ways that He did not originally intend. This is because of Adam's fall from grace, which doomed every part of our being—spirit, soul, and body, to be subject to the *"wages of sin"*. (Romans 6:23)

Sidebar: There is some discussion as to whether our emotions are part of our spirit being, or part of our soulish (aka "the mind") being. The spirit is what is made alive in Christ when we are born again. (*"The Spirit itself beareth witness with our spirit, that we are the children of God."* (Romans 8:16)). The mind must be continually renewed (Romans 12:2). And our bodies will one day rise in Him (I Thessalonians 4:17). However it is generally believed that the mind and personality comprise the soul, and that this is where our emotions reside. We cannot biblically substantiate either position. And for our purposes here, it is actually quite irrelevant. What we can say with certainty is that God has provided us with these emotions. They are integral to who we are, and are therefore part of our redemption through Jesus Christ.

So our spirits, our bodies, and our souls must be redeemed from the curse of sin. Regardless of where our emotions "live", it is clear that God wants to redeem every part of us: "*I pray God your whole spirit and soul and body be preserved blameless unto the coming of our Lord Jesus Christ.*" (I Thessalonians 5:23). This is not an unimportant thing. For if God did not plan for or care about redeeming us wholly, then we should expect to spend eternity in an emotionless Kingdom without any expectation or anticipation of joy, peace, love, or pleasure of being in the Lord's presence.

How absurd! How utterly and absolutely ridiculous!

"*Well done, thou good and faithful servant . . . enter thou into the joy of thy lord.*" (Matthew 25:21)
"*The joy of the LORD is your strength.*" (Nehemiah 8:18)

Well, these verses of scripture pretty much take care of any notion anyone might have about the relative unimportance of our emotions. God did not put into place a grand plan to redeem our spirits, souls, and bodies to eternal life with Him, only to ultimately strip away our ability to passionately enjoy (and show fervent appreciation and enthusiasm for) what He, the Son, and the Holy Spirit have done for us. It is clear that He *wants* us to revel in His glory and presence. How could we do that if we have no emotions to feel that joy with?

So now that we have solidly established that our emotions were made by God, and are important to our life in Him (both now and forever), let us turn back to the references we made earlier about how our emotions, for better or worse, can affect how we feel about our lives and ourselves.

It is life's ups and downs that often direct how we feel at any given moment in time. Great news is worthy of jubilation and joy. But disappointment and anger at negative events that harm, frustrate, or inhibit us work adversely and in the opposite way. Our own sense of self-esteem is usually intricately woven into, and bound up in, these moments of emotional churnings. We succeed, we win, we laugh, and then we feel good about ourselves. We cry, we hurt, we get disappointed, and then we feel negatively about our whole existence.

Sidebar: Our intentions here are not to analyze and evaluate the gravity and importance of one life event against another. The loss of a loved one versus getting that "dream job" are nowhere near equitable for comparative purposes. We know that from firsthand experience. Neither is it our goal to unravel the psychology or physiology of what our minds (and hearts) feel when dealing with the devastating news of terminal illness or a joyous occasion like the birth of a child. Our only offering to those who are in pain is to rely on the Lord to sustain you . . . as we and so many others have. *"For we have not an high priest which cannot be touched with the feeling of our infirmities . . ."*

(Hebrews 4:15) He is well aware of what you are facing in your life. *"Let us therefore come boldly unto the throne of grace, that we may obtain mercy, and find grace to help in time of need."* (Hebrews 4:16)

If we could somehow "strip out" the emotional component to our everyday lives, what would that look like? It's likely that we would have a drab and dull existence, never knowing what it is like to be happy, or to feel sad. Our actions, words, and thoughts would remain unaffected by either adversity or triumph. We could never appreciate being the recipient of a wonderful gift . . . or the giver of one! But if our emotions were suddenly not present, and our world was essentially as it is today, what would happen to water (yes, water)? Would its properties change at all? Would it somehow cease being wet and turn to a powdery or crystalline substance? How about the sun, moon, and stars? Would the sun stop giving its life-sustaining warmth? Would the moon stop orbiting around the earth? Would the stars fail to sparkle in the heavens? Granted, these are all pretty kooky speculations, but for illustration purposes, quite valid and on point. Allow us to explain.

All these things (and more) would be completely and utterly unaffected in this hypothetical scenario. How we *feel* about these things—good, bad, or indifferent—has absolutely no bearing or effect on them at all. They are what they are. They will exist as they were created. They will play their designated roles in God's awesome universe exactly as He ordained. No amount of human happiness, sadness, anger, or anxiety will change anything about them.

As silly as this first seems, it is imperative that we carry this logic one step further—from the natural universe to the supernatural one. Let us overlay our same emotionless existence over a new, yet similar example. How would God Almighty be changed (yes, changed) by the lack of *your* emotions? Would His power and authority be altered or limited? How about the sacrifice that Jesus made at the cross, or the present day ministry of the Holy Spirit? Would Jesus' life, death, and resurrection alter His ability to redeem all of mankind? Would the Holy Spirit be constrained or useless in His ministry? Of course not. Again, and this is truly important to know, how we **feel** about these things—good, bad, or indifferent—has absolutely no bearing or effect on them at all. They are what they are. They will perform as they intended. No amount of human happiness, sadness, anger, or anxiety will change anything about them.

So then, the lesson here is that the supernatural and unseen things are not prevented from fulfilling God's holy purposes and plans merely because of what we feel—good, bad, or indifferent—within ourselves.

Sidebar: The Bible says in Matthew 13:58 that *"He did not many mighty works there because of their unbelief."* Do not make the mistake of thinking that God's plans can be stifled or derailed because of emotion. The key to understanding this is knowing that unbelief is not an emotion; it is a decision about whether one agrees with, supports, or accepts a specific premise. It is a symptom of a lack of faith. Learning about faith—how to get it, maintain it, and use it—is such a complex and elaborate aspect of Christianity that we cannot at all do it any justice here. Please take the time to study faith on your own. It will be well worth your investment of time.

To illustrate how human emotions are neither catalyst, trigger, nor obstacle for God's plans, let us refer back to several examples we have already discussed.

First, Elijah was overly confident, perhaps even to the point of arrogance when he challenged the priests of Baal. He knew that he was God's prophet, and he knew what God was going to do. No doubt his emotions were riding high. Then God did His fiery miracle and proved these things out. Yet, a short time later, the very same Elijah was lonely, tired, and whiny about his situation. He longed for death because he felt like he had failed God. Jezebel had threatened to kill him, and he couldn't cope with the death threats of a single ungodly woman. Thankfully, God ministered to Elijah and helped him recover from his emotional funk. But in the end, God was completely unaffected by his prophet's miserable state. He did what He originally intended, and His goals were never altered or at risk. Eventually, Elijah's self-image and self-worth swung completely from one extreme to the other, and God still fulfilled His plans. As we stated earlier, Elijah ultimately went on to accomplish much more in his ministry, because God was not deterred by his emotional meltdown.

Which one of us has not had an experience similar to Elijah's in that we have gone from the highest pinnacles of self-confidence and self-purpose only to abruptly tumble and crash into the abyss of self-pity and self-doubt? Not a one of us has escaped from such an extreme meltdown in our emotions.

Our next example is the Apostle Paul. Now here was a Christian who experienced danger like perhaps no other before or since. *"Thrice was I beaten with rods, once was I stoned, thrice I suffered shipwreck, a night and a day I have been in the deep . . ."* (2 Corinthians 11:25). He doesn't even reference here how many times he was bound with chains and imprisoned. It is difficult to believe that any *one* of these events would not permanently damage, if not totally destroy, a believer's zeal for spreading the Gospel. Surely, there must have been multiple times that Paul felt lonely, distressed, and *"troubled on every side"* (II Corinthians 4:8). His emotional state had to be fragile from time to time, on the verge of what Elijah experienced at his lowest point. Imagine the effervescent joy of watching God heal a lame man through you (Acts 14:8-10), only to feel the shocking surprise and danger as you're being stoned for doing so. (Acts 14:19) In another instance, you are arrested and roughly escorted to prison, whipped, and bound in chains and stocks, for delivering a woman from an evil spirit. (Acts 16:16-24). The emotional roller coaster would seem to run non-stop for Paul, given his activities and the accompanying dangers and threats. And yet in all these things, God continued to use him, guide him, and instruct him for His own purposes.

We cannot firmly state with scriptural certainty that Paul did or did not have emotional highs and lows. But it is very likely he did. He was a flawed human as we all are. And since we are all made from the same *stuff*—we are all subject to Adam's original sin—we all must be redeemed through Christ—and we all are subjected to the wickedness of the world—it is a pretty sure thing that *sometimes* he felt like we do; lonely, depressed, inadequate, unloved, unlovable, etc. It may be that like Elijah, he longed for death as well. But God saw past all that emotional tumult and restlessness, and forged on with His perfect plan for Paul. While he faced numerous perils throughout his life, his contributions to the Kingdom then, and subsequently all the way throughout history to the present day, are distinct reminders that our feelings have little to do with God's ultimate plans.

Elijah and Paul are premier examples of men whose own self-images, self-assessments, and emotions, were thankfully not the main driving forces in fulfilling their missions for God. The core of the message here is for us to fully realize, and to deliberately embrace, the knowledge that our emotions have little to do with how we should think of ourselves, and by extension, how we fulfill God's perfect plan for us. Stated another way, you and I should *"gird up the loins of your mind, be sober, and hope to the end"* (I Peter 1:13) What we believe and how we feel about ourselves will not diminish God's overall efforts. It can only affect how we make ourselves available to Him.

In the future, let us set aside what often holds us back from pursuing and fulfilling the things of God. *God has esteemed us worthy and capable.* We should not let our fleeting feelings of inadequacy, limited ability, or poor self-image persuade us otherwise.

8

GODLY SELF-ESTEEM
VS. PRIDE

As we learn about how we value ourselves and compare that to how God values us, it may seem interesting, if not unusual, to specifically single out pride from among all the human emotions. We do so because pride is quite possibly the most corrosive and potentially harmful when it comes to our relationship with God—as well as being destructive to our own earthly relationships with friends and family.

There are two types of pride that we must examine. Briefly, the first is pride as an expression or feeling of happiness that one might have for having done a job well; or a feeling of joy towards a loved one when they achieve or acquire something of notable significance through their applied efforts. For example, if you manage to complete a project successfully, or earn a college degree, or get a well-deserved promotion on the job, there is reason to feel elated and happy at this favorable turn of events. But this form of pride is more of an emotional reaction to the sense of accomplishment you and others might feel at a given moment. It is a temporary response which results from a positive event. However, this is not the sense of pride which we must be careful for and wary about.

The sort of pride which we must always guard against is infused with arrogance, selfishness, and even narcissism. It is more of an ongoing and consistent attitude, rather than a briefly soaring reaction to a positive experience.

"Every one that is proud in heart is an abomination to the LORD." (Proverbs 16:5)

"Pride goeth before destruction, and an haughty spirit before a fall." (Proverbs 16:18)

Scripture tells us in these two verses alone, that the latter form of pride is detestable to God. Further, we are warned of ominous consequences that a prideful heart and spirit will eventually lead to and cultivate.

Unfortunately, it is within our old sinful natures to exhibit this pride. Adam first showed it when he disobeyed God by eating the fruit of the Tree of Knowledge. (Genesis 3:6) Either directly or indirectly, he was swayed by the serpent's argument that he would become like God. (Genesis 3:5) It was this prideful notion that allowed Adam to be persuaded, (and actually persuade himself) that willfully engaging in a disobedient act was acceptable.

Sidebar: We are simplifying the event of Adam's disobedience here for reasons of clarity and brevity. The study of Adam's fall is something that every Christian needs to be familiar with and study for themselves. Most important and notable is the fact that Adam's original sin immediately condemned all of mankind to eternal damnation. However, it was Christ's death and resurrection where eternal life and fellowship with the Father was once again restored. (Romans 5:17-19; Hebrews 9:24; I John 2:1)

It is quite interesting to compare the premise of Adam's temptation by the serpent to another passage of scripture in the Bible. (Most Biblical scholars recognize the serpent to be either satan himself, or a willing instrument of satan, but that is not the primary point here.) In short, satan tempted Adam to be like God. In effect, he persuaded Adam with the same prideful idea that he himself had, as seen in Isaiah 14: 12-14. He said, *"I will be like the Most High."* Lucifer/satan deluded himself into believing that he could be God's equal, or even God's superior. That plan didn't work out so well for Lucifer as he and his followers were ultimately expelled from heaven. (Revelations 12:7-9) This haughtiness became problematic for us in that Adam did yield to the exact same temptation; that is, that Adam could become like God if he ate of the forbidden fruit. As we know, Adam's pride got the best of him, and the rest is the history with which we are all acquainted.

That human pride, whether overt or not, exhibits exactly the type of arrogance and narcissism that God warns against in the previously mentioned Proverbs. It is what doomed all of mankind to separation from God. And it did not take too long after Adam's fall before this same attitude of pride would lead to rebellion and the first human murder.

In Genesis chapter 4:2-8, we learn of Adam's two sons, Cain and Abel. Cain was a farmer, whereas Abel was a shepherd. In due time, it was the responsibility of each to make a sacrifice for their covering of sins.

Sidebar: While not specifically explained in this particular passage of scripture, there are many others in the Old and New Testaments that detail how and why a blood sacrifice was required by God. These sacrifices were a foreshadowing of Christ's death for the atonement of our sins. From our vantage point in history, it is awe-inspiring to see and understand that an Old Testament blood sacrifice is a most beautiful and meaningful illustration of God's mercy to us with the gift of Jesus, the Lamb of God, as our substitute. Please study this further for your own spiritual education and edification.

In verse 3, Cain brought of the fruits of his labor from farming as a sacrifice to God. Most likely, it was a quite beautiful assortment of fruits, vegetables, and grains as Cain certainly wanted to offer God his best. But God utterly rejected Cain's offering. Why? Simply put, it was not at all what God required of a sacrifice. Cain's personal pride had convinced him that harvested fruits and vegetables that he had labored for would be acceptable to God as a sacrifice for sin. This was a selfish and arrogant act. He believed that because he took pride in his work, then God should honor that effort equally, and accept the substitution that he had made. What Cain did not understand, was that God, *and only God*, could decide what a satisfactory offering should be. So just like his father before him, Cain had given in to a prideful heart because he had decided that his own decision on an important spiritual matter was greater than God's. *"And the Lord said to Cain, Why art thou wroth? And why is thy countenance fallen? If thou doest well, shalt thou not be accepted?"* (Genesis 4:6-7) Clearly God was not happy with Cain's sacrifice or intentions. He tried to teach Cain the error of his actions. In fact, it seems that God was a little surprised that Cain had been so affected by His response. Of course, He was not at all surprised. He was just trying to teach Cain that there was only one way—*His way*—of offering a sacrifice to cover sin.

Unfortunately, Cain's arrogance wouldn't allow him to repent. Instead, he became angry with his brother, Abel. God had indicated Abel's sacrifice was good, and Cain was jealous of that, so he murdered his own brother out of sinful pride and anger. What a terrible and useless tragedy. Abel died because he did the right thing before God, and Cain was resentful of him, so he killed him. (Doesn't this event somewhat foreshadow the murder of Jesus? Jesus did the right thing before God, and the Jewish clerics were jealous and hated Him for it, so they arranged to kill him.)

In each of these instances with both Adam and Cain, it was the pride of the man that caused them to turn from God and commit a grave sin. As we indicated before, this sort of pride was not derived from a positive or joyful moment or event. It was not a passing "selfless" pride, but rather a loitering "selfish" one. It is a pride that is often introduced into our being by external events and influences. At first sustained and fostered by those influences, it will eventually take root in our own spirit and consciousness; where it continues to grow and fester like an infection. It pervades our thinking and sense of self, and eventually our self-value. We may convince ourselves that it is rooted in healthy self-esteem, but it never is. It is artificial and hollow and has no substance.

King Saul is another perfect example for studying further how human, selfish pride can be the undoing of a person who regularly tries to usurp God's instructions and plans. The Old Testament book of I Samuel details for us the rise and fall of this man who was anointed to be Israel's first earthly king. In Chapter 9, we see in Saul a humble man who truly desires to honor God by honoring His prophet, Samuel. God informed Samuel (I Samuel 9:17) when he first met Saul, that he should be anointed as king. In the verses leading up to this event, and for some time after, Saul was humble, obedient, and spiritually empowered to take on this important role. He esteemed himself as God esteemed him. He did not indulge in foolish or prideful acts. He followed the words and wisdom of God's prophet, Samuel. In Chapter 10, Saul was installed as king and presented to all of Israel. In Chapter 12, Saul was again confirmed by God as king of Israel.

But after a few years of rule, Saul's personality was starting to give in to the pitfalls and luxuries of wealth and power. In Chapter 13, we see Saul's prideful ego begin to manifest itself. He ignores the instructions of God to wait for Samuel's arrival to a battle zone. Instead, he presents an offering to God himself, which was not allowed by anyone other than God's chosen prophet; in this case, Samuel. He then justifies his action by saying that the people of Israel were essentially deserting him, and that Samuel took too long to arrive. (It is at that time that Samuel declares an end to Saul's throne, even though Saul continued his reign of over forty years.)

Another most egregious instance of Saul's prideful disobedience is when he is commanded to utterly destroy the Amalekites in I Samuel, Chapter 15. To summarize, Saul was severely scolded by Samuel (Verses 17-23) for failing to do as he was told. At first, Saul tried to deflect the responsibility away from himself by saying that the people of Israel took the spoils of the Amalekites to present sacrifices unto God. In essence, Saul was saying, "It's not my fault. The people did the wrong, but it was for a good cause anyway." He unsuccessfully tries to absolve himself, and when that doesn't work, he entreats Samuel to fix it for him.

Sidebar: Samuel refuses to pardon Saul's sin. This seems contrary to a loving and forgiving God. After all, Saul sinned and then asked for forgiveness. Shouldn't God have forgiven him? The short answer is that Saul had a history of willfully and intentionally sidestepping and disobeying God's instructions. Also, he never seemed to own up to his mistakes. He consistently tried to shift the blame to anyone other than himself. It was only when his excuses failed that he feigned remorse and regret for his actions. However, God knew Saul's heart. He knew Saul's sorrow was not genuine. That is why God rejected his pleas for forgiveness, and ultimately, rejected Saul as king. The remainder of the book of I Samuel details King Saul's reign without the benefit of God's help and His prophet, Samuel. It also describes David's introduction into the service of Saul, and how he served God and Israel. We suggest you study this book for a more complete understanding of Saul's troubled reign and the introduction of David, who would ultimately supplant him as king.

"Behold, I am against thee, O thou most proud, saith the Lord GOD of hosts." (Jeremiah 50:31)

Pride is not an unforgivable sin. But it is highly destructive. It is a poison which trades Godly self-esteem and the value that He places on us with a self-centered arrogance and haughtiness that destroys our opportunity to effectively serve the Lord. It sabotages our abilities as ambassadors of Christ. It neutralizes our witness. It calls attention to us, usually in a negative way, rather than bring honor and deference to God. Its rewards are carnal and fleeting, and most often lead to other troubles. As shown in Saul's life and as stated in the preceding verse in Jeremiah, God is not going to honor the proud in heart. He is not going to bless, heal, deliver, and promote us if we do not cast off from ourselves the very thing that He hates—***pride***.

"An high look, and a proud heart . . . is sin." (Proverbs 21:4)

Ultimately, it is pure folly for us to revere ourselves so highly. What can we ever do that compares to what God has done, is doing now, or will do in the future? As God berated Job in Chapters 38-41, can we do anything that even comes near to what He has done? Moreover, without Jesus and the Holy Spirit in our lives today, can we save ourselves from eternal damnation? Can we speak a word strictly out of our own strength and authority and heal a blind man, or deliver a demoniac, or restore anything to its former glory? Of course not. *"But Jesus beheld them, and said unto them, 'With men this is impossible; but with God all things are possible'."* (Matthew 19:26)

Sidebar: Science and technology have achieved great and notable strides in every area of life—from food production, to medical advances, to constructing all types of useful and helpful machines and devices, and much more. We do not belittle this, nor do we dismiss it. But we must be clear about where all this knowledge originates. We have what we have, we know what we know, because directly or indirectly God has provided it for us. Simply put, we have "discovered" these things because the Lord has enabled us to do so. We credit Him as the source of all knowledge. He is the Creator of all things (John 1:3, 10), and rightly deserves the honor and praise.

Therefore, we must regard ourselves as He does. We must esteem ourselves as He esteems us. "*For without me ye can do nothing.*" (John 15:5) Foolish human pride is pointless and worthless. It demands to be fed, but it is never satisfied. It expects to be right, but it never is. It demands respect, but it has not earned it. It craves attention, but it never has enough. It never is at peace, nor does it ever enter rest, because it cannot sustain itself. It is hollow, and shallow, and lacks any real substance.

Conversely, legitimate pride is based on our joy in the Lord. It is derived from Him, because He is the source of all things. We can take pleasure in His triumphs. We can take comfort in the fact that Jesus deserves His place of righteousness and glory, and that He is willing to share that position of honor with us. It is that level of esteem that we can rightly partake of—because He is everything—and we are *worth everything*, to Him.

9

GODLY SELF-ESTEEM VS. THE ENEMY

One of the primary objectives in every battle and every war is this: Take away your enemy's confidence, and you can take away your enemy's will to fight. This is also true in spiritual warfare. After studying how willful pride can be so detrimental to our relationship with God, we now examine one of satan's primary weapons to render Christians ineffective. That is, how he tries to destroy our confidence, which can subsequently lead to the destruction of our personal self-esteem.

For most of us, our self-esteem is regularly provided by, or regularly relies upon, something other than how God sees us. A negative turn in our lives can trigger an emotionally downward spiral. Sometimes all too quickly, we become hesitant, ineffective, and uncertain. In the worst case scenarios, we become self-hating and angry, perhaps isolating ourselves from those around us. We may either withdraw emotionally, or lash out at those nearby, particularly against loved ones and close friends. However, these people are not the true instigators of these attacks on our self-confidence and self-esteem. There is another, more likely reason for these spiritual attacks.

"For though we walk in the flesh, we do not war after the flesh; (For the weapons of our warfare are not carnal, but mighty through God to the pulling down of strongholds;) Casting down imaginations, and every high thing that exalteth itself against the knowledge of God, and bringing into captivity every thought to the obedience of Christ." (II Corinthians 10:4-5)

What can the aforementioned "imaginations" do? Why would "high things" exalt themselves against the knowledge of God? Why must "thoughts" be brought into captivity to the obedience of Christ? Because spiritual warfare is also warfare of the mind. Satan attempts to punch holes in your thinking so that you will begin to question and doubt your standing as a Christian. He will try and convince you that you are unsaved and unloved by God because you have failed Him. He will cause you to question and ponder whether or not some sins are permissible, or at least not as offensive as others. Or you could be attacked in your family, your physical body, or your finances; all the while wondering if standing strong is even possible, much less worth it. These assaults are all precisely aimed at a particular objective: your confidence in Christ, and by extension, your self-esteem. If he can eventually sap away your sense of self-worth and your will to fight, then you become less likely to stand against his efforts to wreak havoc.

> Sidebar: Although satan understands he has lost you to the kingdom of Christ, that is not a guarantee that he will leave you alone and move on. In fact, we cite the majority of the New Testament as evidence to prove this notion, since everything beyond the book of Acts was written to, and about, Believers and their growth in Christ. These Books were written to teach, coach, and instruct Christians in all areas of life, while simultaneously recognizing that there is a renegade spirit (satan) in the world, with whom we must contend. Basically, our primary point is that he knows he has lost you, but that does not deter him from trying to render you unsuccessful in your Christian walk and witness. It is his unwavering and steadfast goal to cause you to abandon your efforts to draw others to the Christ the Lord.

We must therefore recognize these attacks as devil-sent, so we can spiritually prepare ourselves to counter and overcome the enemy's tactics. For if we thwart his efforts to diminish our self-esteem and our confidence, then we can stand victorious in other areas of our lives. *"That ye may be able to withstand in the evil day, and having done all, to stand."* (Ephesians 6:13) As Christians, it is our responsibility to stand, but we are not without help as we do so, for we have quite an arsenal at our disposal.

"Resist the devil, and he will flee from you." (James 4:7)

"Behold, I give unto you power . . . over all the power of the enemy." (Luke 10:19)

"Ye are of your father the devil . . . he is a liar, and the father of it." (John 8:44)

"Wherefore God also . . . hath given Him a name which is above every name." (Philippians 2:9)

"At the <u>name of Jesus</u> every knee should bow . . . every tongue should confess that Jesus Christ is Lord, to the glory of God the Father." (Philippians 2:10-11)

"Greater is He that is in you, than he that is in the world." (I John 4:4)

"If God be for us, who can be against us?" (Romans 8:31)

"Finally, my brethren, be strong in the Lord, and in the power of His might." (Ephesians 6:10)

These scriptures directly or indirectly empower us to stand against and overcome the enemy. This is where our confidence lies. This is where the certainty of who we are and Whose we are can be found. We should intentionally and purposefully take our confidence in Him and His Word as the solid and firm foundation upon which we base our self-esteem. As these scriptures indicate or imply, we are to take an active role in repelling the assaults of the enemy. Even Jesus had to say, *"Get thee behind me, satan: for it is written"* (Luke 4:8) The Lord Himself cited scripture to ward off the enemy's temptations. We must actively engage ourselves in the conflict and do the same as He did, if we are to gain the victory.

> Sidebar: Please note that familiarity with Scripture is not the same as having recently and consistently partaken of it. We cannot fuel our bodies by the memories or awareness of past meals—there literally is no useful energy or power in that. Similarly, we cannot fuel our spirits with the memory of Scripture. We must consume God's Word regularly to enable us to draw from the spiritual power it contains.

To ready ourselves for the fight, we take a particular interest in the passage in Ephesians 6:11-18. It begins by instructing us to stand against the *"wiles of the devil"*, and it recognizes that spiritual warfare is the order of the day. In verse 13, we begin to learn that there is spiritual armor with which we should avail ourselves. Each piece is designed by God to fully equip us for the fight before us. We are directed to take them on, and utilize the various components for protection and defense; with the sword specifically to be used as a weapon of aggression against the enemy (*"the sword of the Spirit, which is the Word of God."*).

> Sidebar: Ephesians 6:18 gives clear instruction on how to take the fight directly to the enemy. We should deploy the Word of God by *"Praying always with all prayer and supplication in the Spirit . . ."* (Verse 6:19) Our prayers are the couriers of God's Word—which is *"the sword of the Spirit"*. They help us to strike out at the enemy, and put him on the defensive, rather than us just taking blow after blow without a meaningful and spiritually powerful response.

In spiritual warfare, we must take an active role in our own defense. There is still much to be learned and discussed on this topic, but this should serve as a primer to encourage you to pursue further study. The main purpose here is to call your attention to the fact that the enemy will attempt to deflate your self-esteem by destroying your confidence, and thus render you an ineffective witness for Christ. We must be vigilant, and rely on Godly self-esteem so that we can be prepared and ready for such attacks. Together with the aforementioned spiritual weaponry, we can capably defend ourselves. *"Above all, taking the shield of faith, wherewith ye shall be able to quench all the fiery darts of the wicked."* (Ephesians 6:16)

Our Christian walk is not a passive activity. We must arm ourselves with the spiritual defenses and armaments that God has provided us. We must center our confidence and base our self-esteem on Him, so that we will not buckle in the face of adversity. He is a quite able and capable commander, and He has assured us victory. *"These things I have spoken unto you, that in Me ye might have peace. In the world ye shall have tribulation: but be of good cheer; I have overcome the world."* (John 16:33) Further, He sees that *"in all these things we are more than conquerors through Him that loved us."* (Romans 8:37)

If the Lord Jesus Christ sees us in this way, then that is how we should see ourselves.

10

FINAL THOUGHTS ON GODLY SELF-ESTEEM

Throughout this book we have endeavored to present to you a new way to view yourself. That is, to see yourself as God sees you. We have crafted a compelling case for you to consider because we desire that you be freed from the burdens and negativity of an unhappy and troubled Christian walk. God wants you to be the best that you can be and do the best that you can do—all while honoring Him and the Lord Jesus. He does not desire that you be stifled, or doubtful, or unsure about your standing within yourself or with Him. God wants you to realize your full potential so that you can be a fruitful and productive ambassador for the Kingdom. Then, you can be a light in the world that so desperately needs the Light of Christ.

But be not caught unaware (Galatians 2:4; Jude 1:4). Jesus said, *"In the world ye shall have tribulation: but be of good cheer; I have overcome the world."* (John 16:33)

There *will* be those who persecute you for your steadfastness in Christ.

Nevertheless, Paul gives us all vigorous encouragement beginning in Romans 8:35. *"Who shall separate us from the love of Christ? Shall tribulation, or distress, or persecution, or famine, or nakedness, or peril, or sword?"* Virtually every negative obstacle that the world can produce falls within these broad categories. Please note that he does not say these challenges won't come (as evidenced in verse 36). He says that *they cannot keep us* from Christ's love.

"Nay, in all these things we are more than conquerors through Him that loved us." (Verse 37) Paul states that, through Christ, we are victors over whatever we may face. We win! Because of Christ, we win!

Paul then takes his point as far as he possibly can with what comes next. *"For I am persuaded, that neither death, nor life, nor angels, nor principalities, nor powers, nor things present, nor things to come, nor height, nor depth, nor any other creature, shall be able to separate us from the love of God, which is in Christ Jesus our Lord."* (Romans 8: 38-39)

All of creation, supernatural or natural, God-made or man-made, life here on earth or death itself, angels or demons, things that existed before Paul's time, or things that have been learned or made since—*none* of these can separate us from God's love through Christ. Paul has not excluded anything, in any realm of existence, at any time, or in any place, from his declaration. There is nothing that can ever take us or isolate us from the Lord. With that said, does it not stand to reason that no matter our self-image, our situation, our friends, our family, our finances, our sins, our shortcomings, our physical appearances, our handicaps, etc., that nothing can neutralize nor surpass the power of God's love for us?

To make this more easily understood, let's express this idea in mathematical terms; using the symbol for *"is greater than"* which looks like ">".

The love of God for us through Christ > our lies
The love of God for us through Christ > our sins
The love of God for us through Christ > our past
The love of God for us through Christ > our hurts
The love of God for us through Christ > ourselves
The love of God for us through Christ > our failures
The love of God for us through Christ > our self-esteem
The love of God for us through Christ > our appearances
The love of God for us through Christ > our weaknesses

These all refer to our own internal and personal workings. But to summarize the remainder of creation let us say that:

The love of God for us through Christ > *everything else*

Or we can accentuate this point with one comprehensive and final mathematical reference:

The love of God for us through Christ > *EVERYTHING*

The love of God for us through Christ is greater than everything. So then, there is nothing you can do to make God love you less. There is nothing that exists anywhere that can make God love you less. There is nothing you can *feel* about yourself, or within yourself, that can make God love you less.

Conversely, there is nothing you can do to make God love you more. There is nothing that exists anywhere that can make God love you more. There is nothing you can *feel* about yourself, or within yourself, that can make God love you more.

You may have heard that our God is an infinite God. He knows no bounds. His love for us knows no bounds. His *esteem* for us, or the value He has placed on us, knows no bounds. His sacrifice for us through Jesus was the most, and best, He could possibly give. That is why we can say, with certainty and great confidence

You are worth everything to Him.

Let us reverently honor the Lord, and all that He has done, and all that He is, by taking on, and taking in, how He regards us. Let the self-esteem God has conferred upon us permeate our thoughts and lives so that we can truly serve the Lord Jesus in all that we do and all that we say. Then with newfound hope and revived enthusiasm, like Paul we can *"Press toward the mark for the prize of the high calling . . ."* (Philippians 3:14)

11

YOUR SALVATION: WORTH EVERYTHING

If you are not a Christian (or aren't sure if you are), then this chapter is intended for you.

If you are already a Christian, this chapter still has value for you in that it will affirm what you already know. It may also strengthen your efforts in ministering the Gospel to others.

+++++

"For God so loved the world that He gave His only begotten Son, that whosoever believeth on Him should not perish, but have everlasting life." (John 3:16)

The message of Salvation is quite simple and direct. God is holy and righteous. He created man that way. Then man submitted to evil and became sinful and selfish. *"For all have sinned, and come short of the glory of God."* (Romans 3:23) God cannot truly fellowship with a creature (even one that He Himself made) if it is stained and corrupted by sin. But God did not want to see one of His greatest creations (man) lost from Himself forever. So He set in motion a plan to rescue man from a destiny of eternal damnation.

The plan was to offer a substitute to take on the sins of man. But because it was a man who initially doomed us, it also had to be a man—a different type of man—to provide us a means of escape.

Paul writes of this in I Corinthians 15:45-47 and Romans 5:12-21. The first man, Adam, broke God's law by his willful disobedience to the Father. The second man, Jesus, restored the law by being intentionally and fully obedient to the Father. In fact, in restoring the law, Jesus went even further and made remarkable improvements. He not only died in our place and carried the weight of our sins (while absorbing God's wrath for unrighteousness), He actually rose again to fully implement and legally administrate the acceptance of Himself as our substitute. The Father's requirements for justice and righteousness were now fulfilled. The accuser, satan, cannot at all discount nor diminish the sacrifice Jesus made on our behalf. He cannot accuse Jesus of breaking God's law because He did not. It is now and forever a completed work that cannot be altered or undone by any natural or supernatural force. Man has been restored to full fellowship with the Father because of what the Son did. But that fellowship still comes with one significant stipulation.

You must choose to partake of the sacrifice that Jesus made for you.

You must decide to follow Jesus. You must decide that His sacrifice was for your sake. You must decide to submit to His Lordship. You must decide to accept, without reservation and with complete sincerity, the greatest gift God could have given you—the life, death, and resurrection of His only begotten Son, Jesus.

You may ask yourself "Why?" Why would Jesus do what He did? Why does God care about me? Why do I matter to a Being that I don't even know personally and can't really understand?

The answer is so very simple: because you are *worth everything* to Him.

God created you so He could spend time with you. He wants you as part of His family. He wants to show you off and show off to you. He wants to love you—and He wants you to love Him back—because you *choose* to. You are His greatest creation, and He wants you back in His house so that the two of you can fellowship together forever. You are not just a prize to be won . . . *He created you in His own image.* And you are not just worth something to Him—you are *worth everything* to Him. That is why He has gone through so much effort to win you back to Himself. This opportunity has cost the Father and the Son so very much, and it was all intended so that you and I could be free to make the decision to follow, simply by accepting Jesus. For us, there is no price to pay, there is no installment plan of debt to manage. There is no payment or exchange that we can offer that is comparable to the value of His gift to us. It is absolutely free to those who ask and receive.

Someday, you will more fully understand how the Creator of the universe, the Maker of all that we see and don't see, aligned time, events, and numerous and variable factors to bring you to this very moment. This is the day that may well forge your eternal destiny. This is your opportunity to decide. You alone have this power. No one can make this decision for you. No one can take away your right to decide what to do. You hold the ultimate authority of your own eternal destiny in your hands. Not even God Himself holds this power, for He has given it completely and exclusively to you. It is now time for you to choose, so choose wisely.

If you are willing to partake of the life that God has for you through Jesus Christ, then say the following prayer out loud.

God, I know that I am a sinner. I'm not perfect, and I may not have this whole thing figured out. But I know and understand that Your Son, Jesus, came to earth to live, to die, and to rise again so that I might have eternal life.

I recognize that I am a sinner, and I need to be rescued from sin. I know that Jesus is the Way, the Truth, and the Life, and I ask that You forgive me for all of my sins. I ask that the blood of Jesus wash them all away. I ask that You make me a new person inside—the kind of person You want me to be. Help me to honor You in all that I do and say, from this moment forward.

I accept You, Jesus, as my Lord and Savior. I accept You as my substitute for sin. Thank You for what You have done for me. And I pray that You show me how to know You in a deeper, stronger, and more personal way. Please teach me how to do that.

Thank You for saving me. Thank You for my new life. In Jesus' name I pray. Amen.

These few words, spoken freely and sincerely by you, have now set in motion your path to God's heaven, and eternal life. That life starts here, today. It does not matter if you feel any differently right now. (Praise God if you do!) It does not matter if satan tries to persuade you that these words were meaningless. (If they were, then why would he try to convince you of that?) The only thing that matters is that you have chosen to follow after God and the Lord Jesus Christ. Your name has been written into the Lamb's Book of Life, and your place in God's family is assured.

Now, you must begin to pursue after the things of God. Get a hold of a Bible and begin to read it. Find a Bible-teaching, Bible-believing church and attend services as often as you reasonably can. Remove yourself from (or remove from yourself) any sinful influences around you. And most of all—pray, pray, and then pray some more. That is your opportunity to reach out to God and communicate directly with

Him. He wants to hear from you. Tell Him about every concern or problem you have. Thank Him for saving you and freeing you from the bondage of sin. Let Him know that you are depending on Him to help you learn and mature as a Christian. Ask Him to take care of your needs. Pray for His protection and guidance in all things. And pray for unsaved loved ones who need His forgiveness as much as you once did.

There is so much more to learn and explore about your new life, and if you pursue God, you will learn more about that life, and Him, each and every day.

One word of caution to you as a new Believer in Christ: Like anywhere else in life, there are good people with good intentions as well as those whose intentions are not honorable. As Paul warned in Ephesians 4:14, "Be *no more children, tossed to and fro, and carried about with every wind of doctrine, by the sleight of men, and cunning craftiness, whereby they lie in wait to deceive.*" Basically, Paul is saying to not follow after men or women who profess to know the Bible, but do not work to live and conduct themselves by its standards. Many people may claim to be a Christian, but they are not. Others actually are Christians, but they have never outgrown their own selfish desires and lusts, and are themselves mired in the sinful natures and leanings that they propose to help you out of. Always refer to the Bible, God's Word to us, as the final authority to measure and weigh what others may say about relating to and living for God.

There are so many other things you can look forward to as you progress in your walk with Christ. We are truly and honestly excited for you.

This book is intended to help you understand better how and why God values you so highly, and how you should adapt your thoughts about yourself so that they more closely match how He sees you and what He thinks of you. To the Father, you are a "pearl of great price." Because God Almighty was willing to give the <u>very best</u> of what He had in order to redeem you, you should now know and fully realize that you have tremendous value to Him, the Creator of all things.

You are <u>worth everything</u> to Him.

Let us gladly be the first to say to you, "Dear brother or sister, welcome to the body of Believers. Welcome to your new life in Christ. *"Grace be to you, and peace, from God our Father, and from the Lord Jesus Christ."* (I Corinthians 1:3; II Corinthians 1:2; Galatians 1:3; Ephesians 1:2; Philippians 1:2; II Thessalonians 1:2; Philemon 1:3).

Likewise, we say to you *"The Lord bless thee, and keep thee: The Lord make His face to shine upon thee: and be gracious unto thee: The Lord lift up His countenance upon thee, and give thee peace."* (Numbers 6:24-26)

Finally, we have one more small request that we make to you as a new Believer. Read (or re-read) this book from the beginning. Use your own Bible (we personally prefer the King James or New King James versions, but there are others) to study the points we make in this book. Ask God, in the name of Jesus and by the power of the Holy Spirit, to teach you what you should learn and what you should know. Take the time necessary for your heart and mind to grasp what the Lord is showing you. As you do, your spiritual understanding and personal faith will grow accordingly. You will start to feel differently and speak differently. You will come to treasure the Word, the fellowship of the brethren, and most especially your personal times in prayer with the Lord. You will enjoy a greater sense of purpose in your life and in your actions. You will begin to minister to those around you in ways that are both open and quietly subtle.

Just as importantly, you will begin to realize and appreciate more and more how God sees you. For you are not unimportant. You are not a forgotten stepchild of the Lord. You are the pearl of great price.

To our loving and wonderful Father in heaven, you are truly *worth everything.*

ABOUT THE AUTHOR

FRANK CASSO is married and living in Texas. He and his wife successfully homeschooled three children who are now grown and have entered their own professional and academic careers. Frank has had many years of experience in business as well as in service to his local church. He has also recently co-authored a novel, the first in a science fiction series, with his daughter.